Susan Hilber
Ann Boskath

AN ODYSSEY

FROM

TO

INC.

Susan Hiller (left) and Ann Baskette hold plaque from Arkansas Business *recognizing MOMS, Inc. as the 1992 Arkansas Business of the Year.*

AN ODYSSEY

FROM

TO

Ann Baskette and Susan Hiller

MOMS Valley Press
Little Rock

Published 2001 by MOMS Valley Press,
P. O. Box 241057, Little Rock, AR 72223-0001

All photographs in this book are from the archives
of MOMS, Inc. and are used with permission

Printed in the United States of America

10 9 8 7 6 5 4 3 2 1 HB

ISBN: 0-9712101-0-1
Library of Congress Control Number: 2001118197

Editor: Nancy Russ
Editorial and production team: Jody McNeese Keene,
Ted and Liz Parkhurst, Laura Woodruff, Joy Freeman
Book and cover design: Ira and Carron Hocut

The paper used in this publication meets the minimum
requirements of the American National Standard for Information
Sciences — Permanence of Paper for Printed Library Materials,
ANSI Z39.48–1984.

In memory of:

Susan's husband, C. Frank Dodson, Jr.
and father, Solon B. Sudduth
and Sam

Ann's husband, Bill A. Baskette
and parents, Virginia Morris and Carl E. Barton

and with love and gratitude to:

Susan's mother, Dorothea Sudduth; daughter, Penn Dodson;
husband, Chuck Hiller; and brother, Scott Sudduth

Ann's children, Beverly Baskette Ryan,
Bradley Allen Baskette and Barton Alden Baskette

ACKNOWLEDGMENTS

The events of this story happened because of many people whose lives intersected with ours over the past years. However, we now know full well that, despite the fact that the events did happen, the book would never have become a reality had it not been for the able assistance of our editor, Nancy Russ. She provided not only excellent suggestions but also gentle mediation. The bonus is that we now have a new friend.

Over the years many employees came through the doors at MOMS. Some stayed for but a few days, some for months, but many more for years. Some even came, left, and then returned! Looking back, we realize how God was gracious in providing employees for our needs at hand. Of course, with some we felt He was testing us! Nevertheless, to *all* employees who worked at MOMS and its predecessors, we thank you and honestly say that we could not have done it without you.

We also want to express our appreciation to Judy Fuller, of the North Little Rock Women's Clinic, for having faith in us. To the former owners and original staff of Wallaby Corporation: thank you. You had a great product and a wonderful team. (We never forgot the limo ride!) Lorraine Ferraro, you are such a special lady and dear friend.

Through the years it was necessary for us to seek accounting and legal advice. Two men in particular exhibited ultimate professionalism in assisting us. Even more than that, each took a personal interest in us as a company and as individuals. We will always be grateful for the advice and friendship of Mike Miller and Paul James, both of whom we met early in our careers.

Within the past several years the National Association of Women Business Owners has played an increasingly significant role in our professional and personal lives. As we have become more active in the Central Arkansas Chapter and in national committees, we have not only gained valuable knowledge but also ever more precious friendships. We thank all of our NAWBO friends for their encouragement. One in particular, Kay Werninger, has been our conscience and our cheerleader, from "Have you started your book yet?" to "You go, girls." Thank you, Kay.

We thank the many contacts made through the years and the roles they played individually and often unknowingly in helping to make MOMS what it became.

Susan's Acknowledgments

My daughter Penn and I have often talked about the "sneakies" since the death of my husband—her father. We were able to steel each other at the approach of Christmas, his birthday, and Father's Day, with success, only to be dissolved by a "sneaky": the discovery of a note, the scent of his shirt, the memory of a special time we three were together.

The "sneakies" are back. They reappeared as the finishing touches were being put onto the final chapter of this book. It was no surprise that the first chapters were written through tear-blurred vision, but even now, "my eyes fail because of tears" (Lamentations 2:11). Why? Relief? Yes—it is good to have it finished. Fatigue? Definitely— we set ourselves an aggressive deadline, and met it. Deflation? Undoubtedly—rather like post-partum syndrome, I would imagine. Reflection? Certainly—we are relating the story of the last twenty years of our lives.

Yet it is more than that; it is gratitude. These tears are welling from thanksgiving at the thought of the many people who have influenced, encouraged, and, yes, loved me. I am blessed. Although it would be impossible to list all of their names, some have been especially significant either in the writing of this book, the events described herein, or both. These I want to acknowledge, realizing that there are even so many more, but time and space will not permit.

My dear husband, Chuck Hiller, should have been named Job. When God sent him to me four years ago, neither he nor I had any idea of the turmoil in store. Perhaps we should have had a clue when we celebrated our first anniversary in my hospital room, three days after abdominal surgery. His patience, prayers, encouragement, and precious love have brought me not only through many trying days and nights but also through the joys and challenges related to this book. He probably is looking forward to having a wife back!

The reader will become well acquainted with my daughter, Penn Dodson, whom I love more than life itself. I will need to depend upon the Scriptures again: "Many daughters have done nobly, but you excel them all" (Proverbs 31:29). She is not only the joy of my life but also the one who has inspired and encouraged me to follow my creative pursuits and interests, including this book. Since the final events of this book, our lives have changed once more with her marriage to Elton, her love, her friend, her soulmate.

At ninety-one years of age, my mother, Dorothea Sudduth, is not only my reason for being, a person whom I love deeply, but also one of the best editors and proofreaders for this project. Every day of my life she has been in my corner, encouraging me, cheering for me, challenging me to do my best. She and my father were both such positive influences on my brother and me as we observed their priorities: church, family, education, friends. I am thankful that Mother now lives nearby since we are able to enjoy not only each other but also each other's friends.

Even though brother Scottie is my only true sibling, there are three others who are almost as close to me: his wife Gail, my sister-in-law Wilda, and her husband Bill. I thank all four of these not only for their interest in the book but also their love and friendship. I enjoy being with each one of these people. Having known Wilda's parents, Billie C. and Clay Dodson, from my youth, I always appreciated the love and encouragement they gave to me. Also, I am grateful for the Hiller kids, grandkids, and kids-in-law, all of whom have welcomed me into this wonderful, ever-increasing family.

During the twenty years described in this book, I have become even more mindful of the ways in which my education has prepared me—not for specific events or projects, but for having the confidence to evaluate any situation presented by life, to think about the alternatives available, and to put a decision into motion. To the faculties of Harpeth Hall School, Sweet Briar College and Vanderbilt University I am eternally grateful.

How thankful I am for the many friends who have come into

my life. During the past several months there have been several who have been special influences and provided not only encouragement but also open ears and sage advice. Dottie Minor, Charlotte Tennant, Pam Pariani, Keenan Kelsey, Jane Nelson, and Penn Fullerton are never farther than a phone call away. Finally, I am grateful that God provided Ann as a special friend and co-worker for this Odyssey that He chose for us. She is a special person who immediately brings to mind two songs. One is Carol Burnett's trademark song: "I'm So Glad We Had This Time Together." The second one was recorded by Paul Simon: [We're] "Still Crazy After All These Years."

Ann's Acknowledgments

I would like to acknowledge my husband, Bill Baskette, who taught me how to love all kinds of people unconditionally. He was more concerned with giving than getting and always put others before himself. He lived life to the fullest and expressed more courage in his darkest hours than anyone I have ever known. It was an honor and a privilege to be his wife and his friend.

Soon after Bill's death, I realized that God wished me to use my experience to help others. I have learned that the requirements for answering this call are a willing attitude and a desire to make the right choices. Other necessary skills can be acquired if we keep our eyes on him and wish to follow His will for our lives. I have also learned that each of us has more inner strength than we can imagine when we are put to the test. This book is testament to my belief that we achieve our greatest triumphs through our greatest sufferings.

It is with sincere gratitude that I acknowledge my daughter Beverly for eight years of faithful service as an employee of MOMS. Her decision to leave and become a full-time mother to four children is a worthy one that I admire. Thank you, Beverly, for all of the encouragement that you gave while I was finding my role in society and for teaching me to be a better mom.

I am also grateful to Brad for using the tools of his youth to become a wonderful son and husband and a good father to his children. Despite painful experiences in your youth, you have been able to overcome these circumstances to become a man of character and strength and one who honors your mother and father.

My son Bart has always been a source of joy and happiness in my life. Thank you, Bart, for encouraging me even when I became discouraged and challenging me to continue on the journey. Thank you for your genuine interest in my well-being and happiness.

The memories of my mother and grandfather continue to be a source of inner strength to me. Mother was my mentor, a woman ahead of her time, as evidenced in her career in state government. My grandfather, a county judge in his hometown of Erin, Tennessee, was known as an honest man with much character.

Having been raised in the Little Rock area, I received my education during a most historic time. I graduated from Central High school during the year of the integration crisis. I also attended the University of Arkansas and the University of Little Rock, majoring in Marketing.

Thanks to my many friends who have given me advice and unconditional love. I am especially grateful to my more mature friends of late who always had faith in my abilities: Barbara and Jim Allen, Sue Ward, Debbie Lesieur, Alice Guy, Jeannie Hanson, and my cousin Charlene Barksdale. Finally, I would especially like to thank my business partner and friend, Susan Dodson Hiller. Thanks for all of the memories of the last twenty years. Without your help, the journey could not have been completed. You are one of God's greatest treasures in my life.

CONTENTS

WOMAN OF THE YEAR

Ann speaks:

There we were in the Big Apple, two recently widowed women getting ready to attend the new musical *Woman of the Year*, starring Lauren Bacall. The year was 1981, and it was my very first trip to New York. I was so excited finally to be going to such a famous city. Susan's first trip had been years before, as a wide-eyed thirteen-year-old.

Everyone had warned me that it was difficult to get a good room in New York without paying a fortune. We arrived on the last flight out of St. Louis during an air traffic controllers' strike. We got to La-Guardia at 1:00 A.M., and it was after 2:30 when we finally arrived at our hotel. There was a huge line, and I was sure when we finally checked in that they would tell us our room had been given to someone else. Sure enough, that is exactly what we were told. But, to my surprise, they told us we could have the penthouse suite at the same rate as our reservation. No, that didn't just happen to anyone, especially on the first trip. Perhaps even then I knew that something wonderful was going to happen as a result of our starting a new business just two months before. We had come to New York to attend a computer convention and had already experienced our first success as women business owners by receiving a bargain we had not anticipated.

It seemed fitting that we get tickets to see Lauren Bacall because she too had become widowed and had added many successes to her career after her marriage came to an unexpected end. There we were, just two girls from Little Rock sitting in front row seats of the Palace Theatre ready for the performance of a lifetime, a performance we would reflect on many times as the years passed. Ms. Bacall will never know the impact she had on our new lives and how much in common we shared at that moment.

As the curtain rose we could hear the words, "Ladies and gentlemen, we now come to the moment we've all been waiting for: the presentation of this year's award to Tess Harding!" Here was a woman of substance who had succeeded in a man's world. She seemed to be snubbing her nose at the male figure in her life who had no idea that she could accomplish such great things. It was as though the award ceremony was her opportunity to rub it in his face as the mistress of ceremonies added things like "Gracious, well-known public figure that we all admire" and extolled her as a "pioneer" and "the big cheese" they had come to honor.

As Susan and I sat there in the audience I think we both contemplated what we, too, could accomplish in a male-dominated world of business, especially in the field of computers, which was in its infancy. Would we ever be able to achieve the kind of success that would be recognized in national circles?

It was as though we were thinking, "If she can do it, we can do it." After all, doesn't the first step to success lie in the belief that one can achieve that success? Ms. Bacall, you will never know how much you influenced us back in those early years, even though we were watching a fictional character. Realities are born from dreams and accomplished through hard work. Without realizing it, we were on our way. We, too, would one day become Women of the Year.

Susan speaks:
From the fiftieth floor of the Sheraton Centre, Ann and I looked down onto the blazing lights, antlike little humans, and scurrying yellow rectangular taxi tops that defined Times Square. An elevator ride took us down, down, down, and within minutes we were there in the midst of these lights that seemed to wash down and all around us. Now among the hoards of little ants, we were the ones dodging the scurrying yellow, now three-dimensional, taxis. Fiftieth Street,

Forty-ninth, Forty-eighth, Forty-seventh. Finally, there before us on Broadway between Forty-seventh and Forty-sixth: the famed Palace Theater.

Awe turned to reverence as we first entered its lobby, well aware that decades of celebrities had preceded us into this historic building, on both sides of the footlights. The anticipation intensified as we presented our tickets for the award-winning play *Woman of the Year,* walked down the short aisle, then sidled along a narrow row and settled expectantly into our seats. Most Broadway theaters, including the Palace, are smaller than their fame belies. There is an intimacy that brings the audience right into the play itself. For the moment that had to wait, as the theater's massive red velvet curtain hung before us, a wall of separation between reality and make believe. Trying to maintain patience, we read through the Playbill. "'Playing the Palace'...In its heyday...everyone who was anyone appeared on the great stage: Sarah Bernhardt...Will Rogers, W.C. Fields, Fred Astaire, Fanny Brice, Mae West..." All right here on this stage!

At last, lights dimmed. The orchestra reverberated with exhilarating opening notes of the overture. Then fairly tripping off the instruments came the lilting show melodies. Finally, a drum roll. A brief moment of silence, then slowly, slowly the curtain crept upward until the entire glittering stage spread before us. Gasping was unavoidable.

"Ladies and Gentlemen, we now come to the moment we've all been waiting for: the presentation of this year's award to Tess Harding...Woman of the Year."

Massive applause erupted as Lauren Bacall swept onto the stage with her powerful presence and legendary deep voice. "The ladies are singing my praises, led by the Chairman Pro Tem..."

"What a charge, Kate, in the atmosphere. Fifty bucks a plate for the Woman of the Year..."

"Will you rise, please, as we honor her career in contemporary life as a writer and a fighter and a leader and a wife?"

"...I am...the Woman of the Year!"

Words of praise—big cheese, pioneer, celebrated, admired— all being heaped upon this Woman of the Year. Ann and I were mesmerized, sitting there with tragedies so recently behind us and our brand-new company just established. What a giant of a figure was the stage character Tess, embodied in the equally impressive real-life person of Ms. Bacall. How insignificant we felt in relation to this star, her stage persona, this huge city, this historic theater. Her character's alter ego, the current, somewhat frumpy wife of her ex-husband, expressed it in song: "You're Tess Harding, for [gosh] sake. I've never done anything significant in my life."

At that point neither Ann nor I felt that we had done anything of real importance in our lives, with motherhood the only possible exception. In fact, we were at the other end of the scale—overwhelmed, trying to stay on top of and not under our current circumstances, and wanting to sort out the recent events of our lives that had brought us to this play in this theater in New York City in March of 1981. Would it be possible for us to put the tragic past behind us enough to take our idea and develop it to the point that we really could do something significant in our lives? Would we ever be in a position for people to "honor [our] career[s] in contemporary life?"

SHATTERED LIVES

Susan speaks:

The first several weeks of the year 1980 had been especially enchanting and fulfilling. In February I had watched with pride as my husband, Frank, was inducted into the American Academy of Orthopedic Surgeons. He had worked hard for so many years to achieve this status. College, medical school, internship, residency, private practice, Board exams—all completed successfully. Clay Frank Dodson, Jr., M.D., Fellow AAOS. His future as a prominent physician appeared to have cleared the final hurdle.

The following month, he and I delighted in a combination ski trip/orthopedic conference in Snowbird, Utah. Challenging slopes, excellent snow, edifying lectures, and delectable cuisine fused with a renewal in our marriage relationship to make this a special time. Several months before, we had successfully worked through some situations that had had the potential to destroy that sacred bond. How comforting it was not only to be there in love with my husband, but also to be able to enjoy my favorite sport with a little more abandon than usual, knowing that there were many—some even very famous— orthopedic surgeons on the slopes with me.

"Penn is almost five. I think that we should bring her with us the next time that we come on a ski trip."

On our small farm west of Little Rock, Frank enjoyed being able to leave the cares of patients and operations behind as he bulldozed, built fences, and made hunting knives. In fact, he was accused of being more of a farmer than a doctor. Visitors marveled at his large and well-organized tool collection, saying that the only difference between those and the ones that he used in the operating room was that the latter were sterilized. Saws, hammers, pliers—he used them equally comfortably in his workshop and in the OR.

It was a Sunday afternoon in late April, the month after our ski trip. Our daughter Penn was just getting over a bout with the chicken pox. Only one or two "worsies" still had to be watched so that she wouldn't scratch them, but she was well enough to be outside with us. T-posts needed to be driven to support a barbed wire fence in the barn lot. I held one as Frank operated his tractor outfitted with a post-driver. All went fine until this implement released early, dropping pounds and pounds of heavy metal directly onto my right great toe. Penn stood terrified behind a tree, well aware that something bad had happened. Reacting as a well-trained physician, Frank scooped me up in the front-end loader, deposited me at our door, and began to assess the damage. Great pain, yes, but fortunately no surgery was required, just crutches, bandages, and a big walking boot. Chicken pox, crushed toe—what else?

By the Thursday following the crushed toe incident, I was able to function with crutches and bandages well enough that Frank could take our pickup to an out-of-town auction. The love of auctions came "honest" to Frank since both his mother and father had taken him with them for years and had taught him well. As an adult he became astute and crafty during these sales, often outfitting many of the needs of the farm and family with his purchases.

Besides, one of my dearest friends, Joanne, who then lived in Texas, was visiting us for a few days. She, Penn, and I had a wonderful time seeing friends and just being with each other while Frank was enjoying the challenge of the sale.

"Penn, your mom, Joanne, and I are going out to dinner. It's too late for me to unload the pickup tonight. Tomorrow I will, and I will show you all of the things that I bought. Somewhere down in the load is something I bought for you: a pair of red corduroy overalls. We will get them tomorrow."

Penn never seemed to mind staying with friends or a sitter when we had an "evening out." Our plans that day were for the three of us to meet another couple, Carolyn and Al, for dinner. This was fine with Penn; in fact she was thrilled, since she had stayed with this family before and knew that they had a little boy about her age.

Dinner was especially enjoyable, as we—Joanne, Carolyn, and I—tried to get caught up on years that had passed since we had worked together in a doctor's office. The fellows didn't seem to mind and even appeared amused at our reminiscing, learning about some details that we had neglected to reveal to them before. The entire evening was just a delightful, relaxed time of friendship.

Having played hard, Penn was sound asleep when we picked her up, a rag doll in her dad's arms as he carried her gently to the car and then into her room when we arrived at home. A kiss on a peaceful Penn's forehead, then, "Sleep well, Joanne. We will see you in the morning."

The first few minutes of sleep are so deep and satisfying that any interruption of this normally peaceful state can be disconcerting, but Frank's words were more than that…they were shattering. "Susan, wake up. I have a terrible, terrible headache."

"Ohhhhh—it's getting worse. I'm going to call the ER and have the neurosurgeon on duty meet us there. Ohhhh—I'm feeling so sick!"

"Joanne, wake up."

"Frank, let's go to the hospital now. If you fainted, Joanne and I couldn't get you into the car."

"Susan, you take my car. It is an automatic, and you can drive it with your bandaged foot."

"Frank, please let's get into the car now! Joanne, thank you for staying with Penn. Thank heavens she doesn't have to wake up and experience this. I promise to call."

We got into the vehicle, with Frank feeling worse with each passing minute.

"Susan, this pain is so, so bad that it could really mess me up, even kill me."

"We have been through so much recently that no matter what happens, we can make it, together. I know that you love the Lord, and He will help us."

"Yes, Susan, I want you to know that I love you, I love our baby, and I love the Lord."

"Frank, can you hear me? Speak to me!"

He had slumped and uttered only incoherent mumbles. How could it take this long to get to the hospital? Turn left, then right, then left, then right. Finally the ER dock was in sight. "I have Doctor Dodson. Come quickly!"

That was all that I could do for Frank. He was completely in the hands of the Lord and of this well-trained medical staff. I had delivered him to them, trusting in their competence and skill. Then slyly, gently, almost imperceptibly, the first hint of my future appeared with a mundane, practical task that needed to be accomplished. Other emergencies might need the dock; the car had to be moved. If it was to be done, I had to do it—Frank could not help me. Since in times of crisis it is almost a relief to have something that "has to be done," I did it and then hobbled up the ramp, back to the ER. Good foot— hurt foot—good foot—hurt foot. Slowly. Dazed. Uncomprehending. So few years had passed since he had driven me up to this very same dock and right away found me a wheelchair. "This lady is about to have a baby." How could this be happening at the same place?

I did go on in. Immediately, caring nurses led me to a waiting room, actually to the Doctors' Lounge, empty at this early morning hour. At first I was entirely alone but soon spoke with the neurosurgeon, who needed whatever information I could provide. There wasn't much. He seemed to be completely healthy—then the headache— oh, yes, numbness in one of his arms—then incoherence and collapse.

The diagnosis and prognosis were unclear. All we knew at that point was that he was still unconscious and not responding. I kept thinking, "What if he is...;" "What if he isn't...;" and then "What if he can't..." There were so many possibilities, fears, and even hopes still that it was terribly difficult to tell myself to wait. I even remember talking to myself, "Now, Susan, wait! No, wait. See what the facts are, what the base line is, before trying to answer questions about the rest of your life." Somehow that practice of will brought temporary relief.

The next hours were but a blur. The diagnosis was confirmed: massive cerebral hemorrhage from an unknown cause. Word spread. Friends began to arrive, and one even shouldered the terrible task of informing Frank's parents' minister, who would then break the news to them. My mother arrived within hours. We were allowed ICU visits for just a few minutes every so many hours. My arms were still sore from the continuing use of crutches. Frank was on life support. They took an EEG, then a required second one a few hours later. Their results were the same: flat line—no activity in his brain. Never did I think that I would have to make this decision, especially at age thirty-five. But, yes, on Saturday it had to be done. There was no hope. "Turn it off."

The driveway that led up to our home seemed so long that day. I had not been back since the night I took Frank to the hospital. How could everything still look the same when everything in life was now so different? The trees, the lake, the house...nothing there seemed to have changed, but my life would never be the same. How comforting to be able to throw myself across the bed and sob, alone. Mother, who had been in the same situation only a few years before, understood and stayed away.

Frank's sister and my brother arrived; a multitude of friends were there. Each one was not only immensely supportive but also willing to perceive practical needs and fill them. Sweeping, washing, food preparation—all done. Lists were started as calls, visitors, and notes began pouring in as the news spread further. Blessedly, Penn was shielded from all of this as she stayed with friends and still knew nothing.

There were tasks that only I could perform. I faced so many decisions. "There is not an appropriate casket long enough for him in Little Rock? Not even in Arkansas? Memphis? How long will it take?" All of that was finally settled; arrangements could proceed. How I dreaded the next duty that truly was mine alone.

Penn looked so tiny, perhaps so vulnerable, when she came through the front door of the funeral home. We went into a parlor— just the two of us. I closed the door. She sat on my lap. I took a deep breath, said a quick silent prayer and began. "Penn, the other day your

Daddy got very sick. He was so sick that he did not get well. He died and has now gone to heaven to live with God. In a few minutes we will go into the other room. You will see your Daddy there, but you will only see his body. His soul has already gone up into heaven."

As she reached for a tissue to catch the first of many tears to come she asked, "How did his soul get there?"

"I don't know."

"Maybe a little bird came and took it."

"Yes, a very special little bird."

At times such as this, we try to do everything just right, knowing the potential future impact on a young life. Despite best efforts, it seems that there is always something that goes wrong.

"Mommy, why didn't you want me to touch Daddy's hair when we were in there? Were you afraid that he really wasn't dead?"

Oh, my.

"I tell you what: we will see Daddy again when we get to Tennessee. Then you may touch his hair all you want."

Since medicine had been such a focus of Frank's life and friendships, it was appropriate for us to hold a memorial service in the chapel of the Baptist Medical Center. Physician colleagues, nurses, and staff were able to join his other friends and family to pay him tribute. The minister's words extolled the virtues of working with one's hands. How appropriate this was for Frank, as he used his powerful hands to heal and to toil, equally comfortable with a scalpel and a tree splitter.

Sitting on the plane the next day, surrounded by Penn, Mother, my brother, and Frank's sister, I dared not look out the window. Cargo was still being loaded. I just could not bear the thought of seeing the casket out there. A flight between Little Rock and Nashville takes less than an hour, but part of me did not want this one to end. Finality would have to be faced. Once there, I would no longer be able to pretend that this was just a little drama and that life would return to where it had been the week before. Besides, the next-most-difficult task still lay ahead: Frank's parents.

How does one deal with the premature death of a husband? The tougher question is: how does one cope with the death of a seemingly healthy, successful, wonderful child? I have no idea. The blow must be beyond devastation. Mr. and Mrs. Dodson did cope, however, with dignity and grace.

In small Southern towns, a funeral within a prominent family has customs established over generations. Comfort and sustenance come from miles around as friends and relatives assemble to support each other and to grieve together. By this time it was Tuesday, and four-year-old Penn had been involved in the completely unfamiliar circumstances since Sunday. "No, I think that I won't go to the church." Youthful wisdom often prevails. Several grandmotherly friends were happy to stay with her; nothing could have been accomplished by her going, and there was no reason for her to have the ceremony at the cemetery etched into her memory.

Leaving the gravesite, in the back seat of the car, all I wanted to do was to hug my Mom. That was it; it was over. Perhaps I just wanted to go back and be a little girl again, erasing all that had taken place in the past six days and not wanting to think about what was to be.

I did know that I wanted to get back to Penn as quickly as possible. "She is not even five years old yet. How could she already be fatherless? How can I be both mother and father to her? She is so very precious!"

Even through the devastation of this tragedy a blessing shone through and was readily apparent to us all. Frank had been a tall man, a strong man, an energetic man, at times an impatient man, a vigorous man of many interests. Debilitation would have been a living hell for him. Several days after we returned to Little Rock, our neurosurgeon friend called with unexpected news. The autopsy revealed that the hemorrhage had been caused by a horrific brain tumor—a silent, unknown, stealthy killer that had stayed hidden while growing until it struck its mortal blow by eating into a vital source of lifeblood. Frank had been spared not only the possibility of a life of physical impairment, but also the pain and agony that most certainly would have been his with the advancement of brain cancer. God was gracious. It was tough; it was terrible; but how much worse it could have been!

Ann speaks:

The year was 1980, and my life was filled with the constant activity of a house, husband, and three children. My daughter, Beverly, was a senior in high school and very active in 4-H, a wonderful organization which helps young people build confidence and maturity. My son Brad, in a lower grade of high school, was totally absorbed in football but managed to find time to devote to the 4-H program. Both would later become State and National winners in their categories representing 4-H. My other son Bart was still in grammar school and was active in church activities as well as expressing some interest in the local 4-H program.

My husband, Bill, was an energetic and devoted husband who traveled a great deal in his work but spent every spare moment in activities related to his family. He had coached a girls' softball team when our daughter was younger, and he was active in many church activities, especially those that involved working with children. Although he had become quite successful as a district manager of a national paper company, he never considered his successes in business as important as his successes as a husband and father. Having been separated from his father at the age of two, Bill wanted nothing more than to become an ideal father and pass his love on to his children. Sometimes he even tried too hard, and his expectations were unrealistic. Many of us as parents place unreasonable demands upon our children and simply don't relax enough and have fun with them.

Ours was a marriage of true partnership in every sense of the word. Our talents were in different areas and helped to make the marriage work. Bill had his office in our home and asked that I help him with secretarial duties. I helped him organize his daily activities, which allowed him to concentrate on selling and managing his territory. I was never compensated materially for this, but felt that this was a way I could help my husband succeed. One of the reasons our marriage was a success was the fact that we worked together as partners and were each other's best friends.

Raising children while keeping a marriage stable is one of life's most difficult yet rewarding experiences. I had lived in a couple of foster homes because my mother was a single parent during the war years and child-care was difficult. Perhaps because of this, I loved being a wife and mother and wanted nothing more than to continue that role for many years. I was living a contented life full of love, laughter, tears, and all of the joys and experiences that come with a growing and active family. Because both my husband and I had come from broken homes, we were even more determined to make our marriage work and were looking forward to our twenty-year anniversary in a few months. How could I have imagined that our whole world would be shattered in one brief instant?

It was an extremely hot July, and everyone feared a drought because we had had very little rain that year. My husband was considering a career change and was talking with someone about joining his business as a partner. In fact, he had already written his resignation letter to the company where he had worked for thirteen years. The letter was lying on his desk, and somehow he just had not gotten around to sending it. When I remember the amounts of his doctor bills, I realize that a small company could never have provided the benefits that he had in his present employment. It was perhaps that uncertainty of change that had caused him to delay, but he had vowed that he would do it. Or, perhaps it was God putting the delay in his mind and in his heart. I choose to think that this was the real reason for his delay in sending the letter.

It was late afternoon of that unforgettable day, and I had gone to the dentist's office for a routine examination and cleaning. All three children were at home. My husband and oldest son had been working on a joint project of restoring an older truck, which we had named Dudley. That day the truck had been placed on ramps. The bed was out of the truck, and Brad had been applying a rust remover all day. Bill had been making sales calls and returned home in the afternoon to help with the project. I was sitting in the dentist's chair when a call came from our daughter Beverly. "Dad has been hurt really bad; the truck rolled backward while he was sitting on a stool just below the frame."

I could tell by her voice that the situation was very grave. She urged me to get home as soon as possible. She had already called an ambulance, and it would hopefully be there by the time I arrived. The dentist and his assistant were quite shaken at my sudden departure and expressed much concern in the days that followed.

Everything seemed to happen in slow motion. It took forever to make the fateful drive from the dentist's office. It was as though I was having an out-of-body experience and was watching the events unfold not as a participant, but as an observer. I have since learned that shock does this to us so that we are able to perform tasks that are needed at the time. Otherwise, we couldn't get through certain experiences that require us to use all our energy and presence of mind. I believe it is God's grace that enables us to get through the circumstances in our lives that are the most painful.

After I pulled the car down the long circular driveway in front of our country home, I found my husband lying on the ground sobbing with intense pain. A bedspread was draped over him to keep him from shaking. He said he was cold and couldn't get warm. It was obvious to me that he was in shock. It hurt me so much to see my husband in such pain; it was as though he were a small child, unlike the man that I knew and loved.

I later learned that our son Brad had to move the cab of the truck to relieve the pressure from his Dad's back. I will perhaps never know the depth of emotions that this terrible experience caused my son. An experience like this had the potential of changing him for the rest of his life. He had been extremely close to his father, and they enjoyed doing many projects together. They had a special communication between them and sometimes didn't even have to talk to understand one another. In a school paper written when Brad was seven, he listed "my dad" as the most admired person in his life.

After Brad moved the truck, he enlisted his sister's help in calling an ambulance. She had the presence of mind to call our neighbors, who were retired and active with the Red Cross. She even called the ambulance before calling me. Although she was only eighteen at the time, the wisdom in her decisions was far greater than her chronological years. Because of the training in Red Cross procedures, our neighbors knew how important it was to keep Bill as stable as possible with as little movement as necessary. They placed him on a flat board and held his head carefully to avoid any more injury before the ambulance arrived. It seemed to take forever for the ambulance to appear; we even had to make another call before it arrived. It seems the drivers had gotten lost.

I was kneeling down trying to comfort my husband when the ambulance finally arrived. Bill knew his injury was so serious that he would never be the same; he kept saying he had really "messed up." I, too, felt the gravity of the situation while riding in the back of the ambulance to the hospital. I knew our life would never be like it was before, and I was numb with grief and worry about the future as the ambulance raced to the hospital. I kept hoping this was a bad dream and that we would all eventually wake up and find that nothing had happened. Unfortunately, this was not the case.

When we arrived at the hospital, the doctor on call was the one who had performed knee surgery on my husband a year before. Bill had been particularly fond of him, and they had experienced a great deal of rapport during the surgery and his rehabilitative therapy. Bill became instant friends with anyone he met, and this doctor was no exception. It is ironic that he was the doctor on call when Bill arrived. After a brief examination and a study of the X-rays, he came out and told me that Bill had a serious injury to the spinal cord and would never walk again.

In my heart I knew the injury was serious, but I never thought about the possibility of my husband becoming a paraplegic until that moment. Seeing my reaction, the doctor asked if I was all right. I told him "yes," but I was lying. He just didn't understand. Because my husband was a man of such faith, he would overcome the odds and walk again. The doctor corrected me and said that I didn't understand. It was not physically possible for him to walk again; there had been too much damage to his spinal cord. The doctor told me that he was going to perform the Herrington Rod procedure in a couple of days to stabilize the spine. This would alleviate some of his discomfort and pain. The thought crossed my mind that he could do something miraculous to repair Bill's injury and that the final diagnosis would somehow be changed.

The doctor had been so matter-of-fact in his initial diagnosis, and it seemed like his conversational dialogue had been extremely direct.

I thought that with enough faith, anything was possible. I still believe this is true, but I realize that God chooses the way He answers prayers. We don't understand His way. Everything is according to His will, not ours. I would understand later that the prayer was answered in His own special way.

The next sixteen days at the hospital were like the unfolding of an adventure unlike any I had ever known. Bill had made many friends in his lifetime, and as people heard about his tragedy they poured into the hospital in great numbers. They had to be turned away when there were too many, but Bill saw as many people as his strength would allow. He saw it as an opportunity to witness to others and to share his experience and talk about his love for God. He had participated just two days before his accident in a Sunday School lesson that had emphasized the need to praise God for everything that comes into our lives, even bad things. He later told me that, remembering the lesson, he had done this even in his pain. This is a supreme test of real faith, since it is so difficult to be truly grateful when something comes into our lives that causes us pain or even minor inconvenience.

As Bill was being wheeled to surgery for the procedure on his back, he motioned for me to lean down so I could hear the words he was going to say. He told me that if anything happened to him, he expected me to carry on and to be a source of inspiration for our children. He had told many people that I was his rock, and he wanted to let me know that he wanted this passed on to our children. I shrugged off his comments by saying, "Nothing is going to happen to you." But he insisted and repeated his request. I finally consoled him by saying, "Of course, you know I will do whatever you ask." After all, my children were my greatest joy and treasure in life besides Bill. Then they wheeled him to the operating room.

Fortunately, God had provided a good friend who never left my side during the time of the injury and the surgery. We had been neighbors and friends for a number of years. Our husbands had been the closest of friends. Because my mother was no longer living and because I had no brothers or sisters, friends were a particular blessing to me. In this case, Barbara was the closest thing I had to a sister and a mother. I considered her family. We spent many long hours in the surgery waiting area, and her presence really helped to pass away the endless time. When Bill was finally out of surgery and I was allowed to visit him, I felt very comfortable allowing Barbara to go with me. The first thing we noticed was the fact that Bill possessed such peace and didn't seem to be in as much pain as we had expected. When I asked him how he was feeling, he told me that he was alright, and that he had had a wonderful dream. I was so startled by his answer that I didn't question him at the time. We left the room feeling uplifted by the visit even though it was the direst of circumstances. How could Bill appear so happy and peaceful after undergoing such a serious operation and facing a life in which he would be handicapped? After that, we began to weep and pray for his healing and recovery.

The next few days went by swiftly despite the tragedy, and there was a steady stream of visitors, flowers, and hundreds of cards pouring into the room. Somehow, even the newspaper had picked up the story from the county sheriff's office, and word had spread to various parts of the state. At Bill's request, I put all the cards on the ceiling so he could see them from his rotating bed. He said it made him feel close to those who cared about him and were praying for his recovery.

When he was stronger, he requested that I get a tape recorder so he might make a "love" tape for the church so they would know how he was doing. He looked for every opportunity to serve God even in his limited capacity. Needless to say, there was not a dry eye in the congregation when the tape was played. The minister used this experience to convey to the congregation the power there is in the love of God and how God allows circumstances to be used to move us toward a higher and more supreme level of living. It was as though Bill had been touched by God and was being allowed to live in this supernatural state to minister to others. Little things that would have annoyed him earlier had no effect on him now. He was patient and compassionate toward others, not taking into account what had happened to him. He would occasionally take pain medication, but never the amount the nurses expected him to need. He would always say thank you to them as they came into his room, and it was obvious that they became very attached to him. Each passing day, I was more amazed at his commitment to God.

In the days that followed, Bill began to run a fever and appeared quite ill. I took the time to talk with him about many things, making sure that there were no loose ends to be discussed, and I savored every moment of our time together.

I asked him about the comment he had made in the recovery room about the dream, and urged him to tell me about it. He said he had been in a long tunnel in a wheelchair and people seemed to be laughing at his inability to walk. As he got closer to the light at the end of the tunnel, he began to experience a love that passed all human understanding and was quite unlike anything he had ever known. Bill had always been able to express love to others in a way that I had never seen in other men, so I knew this must have been a powerful feeling that he experienced. He was known to hug his friends, both men and women, and often told them he loved them. Everyone knew his heart was as big as his body, and they came to accept this as part of his overall personality. His recounting of the tunnel experience greatly moved me. I found myself at a loss for words as he described it.

Many people explain this as a near-death experience, and scientific people will tell you that it is a chemical reaction in the brain caused by trauma. I believe it was a revelation from God. Nothing else could explain his physical state and his newfound sense of peace and joy. It lasted far beyond the experience of the dream.

I am convinced Bill was allowed to preview heaven in a way that most of us will never experience. It was as if he was allowed to remain on earth in his bodily form, but his heart and mind were already in heaven. I wept as I heard his description of what this experience had meant to him. Later that evening, his mother and father, who had been divorced for many years, both came into his hospital room. His father offered to leave. Bill asked him to stay so that both of them could be present as he thanked them for the love they had given him and told them what they had meant to him. At that point, neither of them wanted to leave, despite the negative feelings that their divorce produced towards each other. It no longer mattered what their personal feelings were, only that they were seeing their son in a debilitated state, being nothing but a wonderful and loving son far beyond what they deserved.

Somehow Bill made it through the night and appeared to be overcoming the fever and feeling stronger. I was very hopeful that he would get better, and we began to talk about his rehabilitation period. The spinal cord injury center had talked with us about sending him to a hospital that specialized in this kind of injury. Their goal was to get him back into the mainstream of society again. In the early afternoon, a neighbor came in to visit him, and I decided to go to the waiting room and visit with our daughter, Beverly. Since I felt so many times during Bill's hospital stay that I was neglecting my children, I welcomed any time I was able to be with them. We were sitting and talking when the neighbor, Bob, came running out and told us that Bill had had a seizure. He recounted that Bill was laughing about looking like a grizzly bear since he had not had a shave in a few days, then suddenly he was unable to breathe. The terrified neighbor ran to the nurse's station, and a crashcart headed to his room. I had heard the Code Blue announcement but didn't give it much thought until Bob ran to find us. I tried to go into Bill's room, but the nurses prevented me from entering.

The autopsy indicated that a clot had formed the day of the injury. This pulmonary embolus had dislodged and gone to his lungs, ending his life. The next time I saw my husband, he was no longer living. I didn't stay long in the room because we had made our peace the day before. There were no unresolved issues. I thank God for giving us that precious time together.

Our minister and his wife had gone to Hong Kong for a mission trip, and they later called to give me their sympathies and condolences. Their son conducted Bill's funeral, the first which he had officiated. Over nine hundred people attended my husband's funeral, which was a testimony to the type of life Bill had lived. He had friends from every walk of life, and people had always been attracted to his zest for living and his love of life. He made everyone feel that he or she was the most important person in the world when they were with him. Quite naturally, he had an abundance of friends. I received many letters from people he had stopped to help in their time of need, which explained why he was often late for dinner. The letters were always the same, "You don't know me, but your husband helped me…"

Bill left his mark in his forty-two years of life and left a wonderful legacy of love for his family to hold dear to their hearts. To this day, I am still very close to all of my children and try never to let any disagreement or difference come between us. No difference is so important that it cannot be worked out through compromise. A family is the greatest treasure God gives us, and he binds us together in love and commitment to each other. We are commanded to love one another unconditionally, despite our differences, because our family ties were carefully arranged by Him.

The days after the funeral were filled with continued outpourings of love and letters of sympathy. I felt that God was giving me a special grace, and I related in a new way to the hymn entitled "Love Lifted Me." Never once was I angry at God, because I knew that God had a special plan for my life. Not too long after Bill's death, the revelation occurred to me that God had answered my most fervent prayer: Bill was walking again, this time in heaven with our precious Lord. It was now time for me to move on, to discover what God had in store for my life and the lives of my children.

TOWARD RECOVERY

Ann speaks:

Soon after the death of my husband, it became apparent to me that God had used the experience of Bill's death in a miraculous way and that I was responsible for passing on this experience to others. I have always believed that God wants us to be communicative individuals, and that means that we are to share our experiences with others. By so doing, we can provide a blueprint to other people in similar circumstances. Just as we need a road map to get to a destination, discussing an experience with others can help us avoid getting off track and losing our perspective in a difficult situation.

Because I was widowed at an earlier age than most women, I longed to have the support of other people in like circumstances. I had faced the death of my mother when I was thirty; however, there was no one with whom to communicate. It was a tremendous burden that both of us carried. My mother had cancer, and it was terminal. Her strong faith and belief in God strengthened us and somehow we both muddled through. It would have been so much easier if we had been able to verbalize this experience to others who had experienced death and the journey of a terminal illness.

For advice on how to give and get support, I went to one of my husband's closest friends, Jim, who was in the insurance industry. I knew he had dealt with delivering insurance checks to survivors of the deceased. After much research, he only found programs available through AARP, and they were geared to senior citizens. Since being widowed at a young age usually involves raising children, my inner sense told me that the kinds of situations and problems faced by younger people are quite different from those of senior citizens. Jim's research did uncover a national organization located in Pittsburgh, Pennsylvania, that had been founded for young and middle-aged people.

The name of the organization was THEOS, the Greek word for God. The letters THEOS stand for "They Help Each Other Spiritually." The group had been founded in 1962 by a widow named Bea Decker. Jim and I both felt encouraged by the fact that there was an organization out there geared toward the needs of younger widowed persons. Unfortunately, there was not a local arm of this group in Arkansas. Since there was no representation here, it occurred to us that we should start a local chapter.

A few days after we began getting information on THEOS, I received a precious note in the mail from a young widow. The note began, "Even though you don't know me, I wanted to write and let you know that you and your family are truly in my thoughts and prayers at this time." The note was dated August 18, just eleven days after the death of my husband. The author of this note, Susan Dodson, had no idea that I immediately recognized her name and that I even felt that I knew her.

In April of that same year, I had been working for five very busy pediatricians at a local clinic. One day, we referred a child with a broken arm to an orthopedic clinic. I distinctly remember talking to Dr. Frank Dodson, the orthopedic who was on call. He suggested that we send the boy to the local hospital for X-rays and treatment. A week later we received a thank you letter for the referral of this child. Doctors usually do this as a courtesy; however, Dr. Dodson had died over the weekend. All of us at the clinic were saddened by the loss. We had just read the obituary in the local paper and knew that the thirty-five-year-old orthopedic surgeon had left a widow named Susan and a five-year-old daughter named Penn.

God truly works in mysterious ways. Without our even being aware of it, He links us to other people with invisible threads. God had provided a person with whom I could form a healing relationship and fulfill the mission of THEOS, "they help each other spiritually." I took this as a serious sign that God was calling me to organize a local chapter and had provided another person in like circumstances to help me. In the Bible, God frequently provided a helper to someone who was to fulfill a mission. A case in point is that Paul was given Barnabas to help him in his ministry. The term "two are better than one" is profoundly true and is indicated many times throughout the Bible.

Soon after receiving the note from Susan, I called her to thank her for her healing words. I told her that I had not met her former husband, but that I had talked with him on the phone. I also told her about the possible formation of THEOS in our area and asked her if she would like to help in this endeavor. She immediately responded "yes," and because of this, we set a time to meet at our local church. In the initial discussion, I discovered that we both attended the same church and both lived in the Ferndale area. This was further confirmation that God had linked us together. We also discovered that our husbands had met a few months earlier, and I even found out that she and her husband had bought a house and acreage just five miles from our home. Bill and I had looked at this same house to buy. Because the size did not meet the needs of a family with three children and renovation would have been costly, we built a two-story house in the area. I was amazed that Susan and I had never met, but I believe that God only intended us to meet after we had both suffered great losses, and it was in his timing to do so.

Now that the idea of a local THEOS chapter was becoming more concrete and there were now two people instead of one to establish it, there was a lot of organizational work to be done in order to make it a reality. One of the first things I did was to contact the religious editor in our area to see if he would be interested in interviewing us and learning more about the ideas we had to form a local chapter in our community. Much to my surprise, he was interested and even ran a feature article in the newspaper in September. As a result of the article, another reporter called us to run a similar article in a competing newspaper. After that, we were called upon to make presentations at some of the local churches. I was even given an opportunity to appear on a couple of local television stations and communicated that the first chapter meeting was to be held November 12, 1980. Behind the scenes but with no less importance, Bill's friend Jim was making contacts with the national organization and getting all of the preliminary details taken care of to establish a charter for our new chapter. He even provided the charter fee to help in its establishment.

In all our contacts and attempts at publicity for THEOS, we kept stressing the idea that the uniqueness of this group was that it was geared toward young and middle-aged widowed persons, both male and female. We wanted to make sure that everyone understood that there was a certain age group we were trying to reach. Finally, the day of our first meeting approached. This was to be held at the First Baptist Church in Little Rock. It was the church we both attended, and they were happy to donate a room for us. They even provided coffee. To our amazement, twenty-five people in the targeted age group attended the first meeting. I knew then that the dream had become a reality. God had forged a mission, provided willing servants, and this mission was on course to being fulfilled.

Soon after our first meeting, when word began to spread about the support group, Baptist Hospital contacted us about a Hospice program for their facility. They invited us to jointly participate in a presentation to the staff. Not long after that presentation, they decided to form the Hospice program which is still an active and thriving ministry today. They asked if they could work with us on a referral basis, sending several individuals who were facing widowhood in the very near future. I had always felt that Susan's and my circumstances were part of God's plan surrounding our husbands' deaths and our newly formed friendship, but I realized that the plan was on an even grander scale. How wonderful it is to be a part of such a large force when God decides to move. Even though I was an unworthy vessel, God had picked me to help coordinate the efforts of both the THEOS and the Hospice programs and bring them to fruition. My husband's death had not been in vain; instead, his death was the inspiration for all of this to happen. I know Susan felt the depth of this movement as well and had similar emotions.

Since THEOS is a national organization, they provided resource materials for our monthly programs to meet the needs of recently widowed individuals. Rather than the meetings being depressing and morose, they were informational and provided tools that all of us needed to consider in establishing our new lives and our new roles in society. Members felt at home in THEOS and could openly share their insecurities and fears for the future. Each of the members was requested to understand and memorize the ten stages of grief in order to learn to cope in a more effective way. The ten stages of grief follow.

- **Shock**—The first stage may last a few days or a few weeks. God apparently has built in this safety device, because it allows a temporary escape from reality.
- **Emotional confusion**—Sometimes emotions are so painful that you cannot believe that anyone understands them. There is no real focus in day-to-day activities and not much is accomplished.
- **Depression and loneliness**—This is when the reality begins to set in and dark clouds come between you and the sun. Sometimes it feels like you are in a dark pit and there is no light at the end of the tunnel.
- **Physical symptoms**—You experience dulled senses and difficult breathing. Sometimes an individual uses an escape such as alcohol or prescription medicine in order to get through the day.
- **Panic**—There is often fear of many things, including a loss of security and a loss of the power of concentration. These fears are usually unwarranted.
- **Guilt**—This may be normal guilt but sometimes it is neurotic guilt. It may occur because we feel we didn't do all we could for our spouse or failed them in some way when they were living.
- **Anger**—Angry feelings are normal. The focus can be a person or God. Sometimes these feelings are repressed, but they are normal. It is important to deal with them and work through them.

- **Return to normalcy is slow**—People may ask you to be
  your "old" self when the truth is, you will never be the same.
  Some feelings of the "old" self can begin to emerge.
- **Hope**—This is when feelings of confusion, anger, panic and
  guilt begin to diminish and you begin to feel human again.
  The clouds begin to be lifted from your soul.
- **Adjustment**—You start to be able to accomplish things and
  bear fruit in your life. Whether you are healthier and happier
  or weaker and sicker depends on the way you have handled
  your grief.

The ten stages of grief may not come to everyone in this exact
order. Sometimes the grief stages can overlap one another. It is also
not uncommon to repeat a stage. The grief cycle can continue for
several years if the individual does not allow himself to heal properly and to face emotions as they occur and realize that they are normal. Repressing one's emotions can only delay rehabilitation.

Once widowed persons begin to understand the grief cycle, it
is easier to adjust and become an effective member of society again.
Anything that we know more about improves our chances of rehabilitation and recovery to live a new and different life. In many cases,
individuals can become stronger and live even more meaningful lives
as a result of going through this tragedy.

Mosaics are a very beautiful art form, but they are made up of
broken glass. We too, can become beautiful works of art through our
brokenness. Sometimes it is through our greatest suffering that we
can understand and appreciate the truly important blessings of life
and learn to keep our priorities in the right order.

During the three years that Susan and I were officers of the local chapter, three other chapters were formed in Arkansas. Today, two
of the original chapters are still in existence, and THEOS is listed as a
reference through many outreach services. While we were involved
in our chapter, over two hundred fifty widowed individuals were in
attendance. The ministry was meant to be a rehabilitative type of support group, and it is quite natural for there to be much attrition in
membership and new people in attendance.

It is gratifying to remember that many souls were made stronger through relationships with others in similar circumstances. There were even some marriages that occurred as a result of attending the meetings, although that was never the focus of the meetings. It is interesting to note that most men remarry very quickly, and most women do not. That is probably due to the fact that women are more diversified in their interests and their emotional makeup. Since women bear children, they have to learn to become adaptable to more situations and conditions. No one is ever truly prepared to experience the death of a loved one. Thank God our society has provided more avenues of education and help through communicative efforts such as THEOS and other support groups.

One evening when our speaker for the evening was prevented from attending, I decided to have a different kind of meeting. I challenged everyone to think of at least one benefit of being single. At first this was not very well received, especially by the people whose memories of their spouses were very fresh due to recent deaths. I asked everyone to humor me and just try to think of something to say that would make themselves and others feel better. I never will forget that a particular woman with tears in her eyes stood up and said, "No more Howard Cosell on Monday night." Another lady said that she didn't have to change the bedsheets as often because she switched sides of the bed after one week. This allowed her to go two weeks without laundering the sheets. Because laughter had erupted in the midst of pain, before the evening was over we all had a new ray of hope in our lives. This was an example of the healing that takes place when we allow others to share our thoughts and our burdens. Thank God for Christian support groups because they lift spirits and put together broken lives.

As Susan and I worked together in the THEOS ministry and we each thought about where our place in society might be, God opened an avenue for us to consider. It is said that when "God closes a door, he opens a window." The idea of starting a business was already being formed without our conscious knowledge. Through teamwork efforts in THEOS, it became clear to both of us that we were a pretty good team. It remained to be seen where this would lead.

"DON'T JUST DREAM ABOUT IT"

4

Susan speaks:

The THEOS ministry, off to a great start, had not only provided solace and inspiration to its increasing numbers but had also allowed Ann and me to mourn in a safe, supportive environment. Grief is a blanket that not only envelops and comforts, but also forms a cocoon of isolation.

"I am safe as long as I stay right here," is the thinking.

Grief, especially following the death of a spouse, is an accepted emotion, one that is provided credence and latitude.

"As long as I am grieving actively, I don't have to deal with the rest of the world. Everyone understands."

Despite the positive strides that we were making through our work in THEOS and the precious support given by our families, we were still grieving actively and intensely, but privately and individually as well.

For each other, we tried to put forward the best foot. To the world, we were "coping so very well." Inwardly, we wanted to scream and rant about the unfairness of our plights.

I wondered, "Why is this welfare recipient on lower Seventh Avenue still alive, and my husband—who had such a brilliant surgical career ahead of him—is dead? Dead...dead?"

Ann told me, "Bill wanted so badly to have a bunch of kids and a happy family to contrast the painful divorce of his childhood. There are so many deadbeat dads. He loved his children and was providing a wonderful home for us all. Why did he have to die? Die...die?"

Evidently, we both were continuing to work through the Whys. We were still wrapped in grief. However, this cocoon of isolation was also the cocoon of preparation. We were gathering strength as we were healing.

In a THEOS program we illustrated one significant effect of the death of a spouse by using two wooden blocks, each about two inches by four inches by eight inches long. We stood the blocks vertically, propped one against the other and then removed one. Of course, the other promptly fell. I saw several lessons in that demonstration. One was that no matter how self-sufficient either spouse is in a marriage, each depends upon the other to provide the completion of a unit that is viewed by society, by the community at large, as "a couple." When one is removed, that unit is no longer there. The survivor is forced to confront the fact that "I am no longer part of a couple."

"What is my new designation? What will be my new role in society, in this community?" A grieving widow has many questions.

It was not surprising that I had become a doctor's wife. Not only were my grandfather and brother both doctors, but before the proposal of marriage from pre-medical student Frank, I had even considered entering the profession (but decided that one doctor in a marriage is enough). By April 1981, I had actually been the wife of a medical student or bona fide M.D. for almost fourteen years. Society identifies that role. Suddenly, though, that title had been stripped from me.

Ann loved being the mother of three children. She was very active in PTA, 4-H, and all their other activities. However, she was not only a mother but also the adored wife of a successful businessman, and she provided backing and encouragement in his professional endeavors. Most of their friends were couples—from church, from his company, even from their children's activities. They loved having friends nearby. In an instant her role was changed. She was no longer a wife, no longer part of a couple.

What would our future roles be? Sure, we were still mothers, that didn't change. Still in that protective cocoon of grief, we began to evaluate what our lives would hold in the next phase that was fast approaching.

At the time of Bill's death, Ann was working in a pediatric clinic. Soon after Frank died I was offered and accepted a job in the office of a surgeon who was also a friend. These jobs were neither challenging nor taxing, but they provided another raison d'être for each of us. Our children could watch our willingness to reenter the work force. They could see that we were trying to go on. From their perspectives of ages five through eighteen, they probably thought that we were doing fine.

Considering…well, yes…considering…we were. However, we wondered with singer Peggy Lee who posed the question: "Is that all there is?"

No.

During the work with THEOS, it became obvious that Ann and I not only had very dissimilar personalities but also possessed different talents and attributes. In fact, as the weeks progressed we realized that these areas of expertise were not only different but also complementary. Ann has always enjoyed being the administrator/organizer. One project undertaken from beginning to end and done well brings her great satisfaction. By contrast, I prefer to have in hand a number of simultaneous ventures in varying degrees of completion. For Ann, the greatest joy lies in the conclusion of the task—all in a box and tied with a ribbon. For me, it is the brainstorming, the design, the beginning that is the most fun.

Yes, our personalities really are quite different. Succinctly, Ann tends to be more uptight while I tend to be more laid back. The positions of the driver's seats of each of our cars are even an indicator. Ann's is almost upright, with her knees fairly touching the steering wheel. Mine? Tilted back at a significant angle. Typically, Ann's desk is neat and tidy; mine is…shall we say, creatively organized, usually by the pile style.

Did all of this portend success or potential failure?

Frankly, at that point, we had not thought of either since "the idea" had not yet emerged. We were still in the protective, nurturing cocoon. However, the longer we worked within the THEOS organization, the more we embraced its symbol, the butterfly. There began to be stirrings within that shell. We began to assess the situation with newfound honesty and an emerging sense of direction. Continued leadership involvement with THEOS enabled us finally to face unexpected reality:

- We were different but complementary.
- We worked well together.
- We each had a strong Christian faith.
- We shared a firm belief in the "do right rule."
- We each needed to establish a new role in society and the community.
- We both had young, dependent children at home.
- We were to be the ones to provide for them.
- We really did want to embark on a career.
- We were both young and energetic enough to take on some kind of venture.
- We each had enough inherited money to help us get started, but not enough to sustain us along with our families for the long haul.
- It was time to get started.

So, our minds were in harmony. We wanted to "start a business." Oh, that sounded rather glamorous and not so difficult. However, the focus and direction were not immediately clear. Ann's husband and father had both been in sales and marketing, and she had been closely involved with Bill's career, assisting him as he maintained an office in their home. Just before he died, they had even discussed forming a business of their own. During Frank's three years in medical school, I worked at St. Jude Hospital in the biochemical research department. Two subsequent Navy years found us in Florida, where I was trained and then worked as a computer programmer and systems analyst. When we moved to Little Rock, my focus shifted to medical office management after I accepted a position as manager of an orthopedic clinic. Having a computer in a medical office was highly unusual in the early 1970s. Nevertheless, it sounded like a great idea, and soon we had one.

Sales—computers; computers—sales. Would it be possible—feasible—for us to sell something that dealt with computers? Programs? The computers themselves? A combination of both? That butterfly was, indeed, beginning to stretch its wings.

It was time for advice. Whom could we trust to give us honest counsel? Someone who hopefully would not laugh in our faces but at the same time would be straightforward with us. When Ann suggested the friend who had helped us found THEOS, the choice was made. He not only knew us both well by then, but also had had several years in business for himself. In fact, he even appeared flattered that we would come to him when we called for an appointment.

"Jim, we have this idea but don't quite have all of the details worked out."

The session continued as the three of us became more enthusiastic about the project and its possibilities as various ideas were thrown out then bantered about. As a practical businessman, Jim provided sage advice about the mechanics and even some pitfalls of the business world.

Our meeting became quite lengthy, and Ann left the room to go to the ladies' room. When she returned, it was my turn. I almost ran back to the conference room and even interrupted Jim by saying, "Ann, did you see that magazine in the ladies' room? Did you see the article that was opened? Did you see the title?"

"Don't Just Dream About It; Do It!"

From that moment on, we had no doubt that God had wanted us to establish this business. We were not just to dream about it; we were to do it! He had not given us many details, but we didn't need any more that day. We knew without a shadow of a doubt that this was the plan for our careers and that He would provide the direction to make it happen.

This incident reminded me of a sermon excerpt from the past. Someone asked a noted theologian if he felt that he had enough of God's grace to be able to withstand being burned at the stake, as had martyrs in the past. This wise man retorted, "No, I just have enough of God's grace to allow me to make it through this conference here in Indianapolis."

God had provided daily grace to enable us to survive the losses of our husbands. Then He planted the idea of a business into our minds. He graciously had provided affirmation with the magazine article title. We knew that He would supply not only the grace but also the wisdom, direction, and strength to continue.

Just down the road from Ann's home there was a dog that was a car-chaser. He would crouch beside the roadway...lower, lower, trying to become invisible to the aluminum, steel, and plastic adversary as it approached...extend, pounce forward, then run, run, run, barking furiously trying to equal or surpass the speed of this superior beast. What would happen if that dog ever did catch the car...what would he do with it?

We had caught the monster; now what to do with it? Following our meeting with Jim, we proceeded with haste toward the official incorporation of our idea into a real business entity. Sitting in the lawyer's office, we hardly knew what to think about all that was happening, but we both kept returning mentally to that magazine article in the ladies' room at Jim's office. It still felt like a dream, but we were no longer just dreaming...we were doing!

An S-Corporation instead of a C-Corp? That sounded reasonable after the explanations of both. Officers? This was a defining moment in our future relationship. We knew that the corporation needed a President and a Vice-President. It also needed a Secretary-Treasurer. There were only two of us to fill all of these positions. Had either of us been egotistical or power hungry, we would have fought for a specific title. Not so. It was decided quickly and easily that Ann would be President and that I would take on the other titles.

Name? We had that covered since we had thought about the idea a lot before going to the lawyer's office. By this time we had worked diligently to develop our initial plans and strategies. Indeed, we thought we were going to combine our experiences in marketing and computers. We would write and sell custom programs for businesses. Since only a very few of this type of business were on the market at the time, there seemed to be no reason why we couldn't develop another one.

Our goals really were quite lofty, much more so than we had ever imagined. In line with our imposing aspirations, we came upon a rather grand name: Custom Software Consultants. With the assurance that this project had been ordained and was being directed by our Lord, we designed an excellent logo. The letters CSC were vertical, with the first two overlapping just so that they would form a stylized fish, the universal symbol of Christianity. We even added a small dot for the eye of the fish. This was to be a subtle message of our beliefs to the world.

"Sign here, each of you."

"Done!"

Ann L. Baskette, President, and Susan S. Dodson, Vice-President, of Custom Software Consultants, Inc.

We felt quite proud of ourselves at that point in time. There we were, corporate executives. We had formed our own business. It felt good to be able to reply when someone asked, "What are you doing?"

"We have our own company, Custom Software Consultants." At that moment we would confidently pull out our new gray, black, and red official business cards. However, our egos and the temporary inflation of self-worth were brought into perspective when we realized that some of our friends thought that we were going into the *lingerie* business.

"No, not that kind of soft wear—computer software, you know, the programs that make the computers work."

Even when people understood a little more about the business, it was evident that many of them were not taking us seriously. We knew that some of them felt that this little venture would be good therapy after all we had been through. Besides, it would give us something to do with our time when we weren't looking after the children.

They evidently didn't realize that we were in the state of mind and action described by another song, a Helen Reddy hit: "I am woman, hear me roar!"

EXPERIMENTAL–OBSOLETE

5

Susan speaks:

Since by May of 1981 our fledgling business had developed some sense of direction, it became evident that both Ann and I needed to find out more about our chosen industry. Just days after incorporation, we noticed the announcement of a Radio Shack Computer Show, which was to be held in Little Rock. We were there! As those sponsoring the show had planned, we were further inspired to attend a Radio Shack computer course, given at the local dealer's store. The course was very limited in scope but somewhat helpful.

Then our first really intensive sashay into the realm of computer education was a programming course at the local university. That was of absolutely no good at all. I should have known that a course in COBOL would not have helped us at that point in time. Ann doesn't mind my saying that she was completely lost in the course. She said that she felt that the instructor was speaking a foreign language. Just as in life it is important to figure out what one wants to do, it is also important to determine what one does *not* want to do. To find the right road, quite a few wrong ones may have to be eliminated. It became evident very quickly that Ann's future did not lie in the field of programming. I decided to continue, however.

Mother was visiting us for several weeks that June to stay with Penn while I attended classes. One morning I was either frustrated about the content of the course, late for the class—or perhaps both. A cup of fresh, piping hot coffee in hand, I put the car in reverse and pulled out of the carport, just as I had done almost every day for the past several years. In my haste, not only was I going faster than usual, even in reverse, but also had not taken time to notice the tractor and Bush Hog parked in the area normally used as a turnaround. *Thud*! *Splash*! Owwwww! A cotton blouse offers very little protection against hot, hot coffee. My chest was burning, but my self-directed temper even more so.

"How could I have been in *that* much of a hurry and have been *that stupid*?"

Fortunately, the burn was superficial, and the car barely damaged. Of course, the Bush Hog didn't even show any evidence of the collision, welded beast that it is. Also, luckily since the course was only one month long, soon that torment was over. Looking back I realize that it wasn't the course itself that was so torturous. I was still confused and frustrated, trying to deal not only with lingering grief but also the conflicting pressures of child- and work-related activities. Having to drive to the University for either classes or computer labs and then feeling that the course content was not targeted to my current needs evidently made me resent the time spent away from my daughter and the fledgling business.

I have no idea how we found it, but soon after the COBOL fiasco one of us discovered information about a computer conference that sounded like it would be very helpful to us. To be honest, almost any information would have been helpful at that point. Not only were we impressed with the content of the conference, but we were especially happy to see that it was to be held in New York City—not in some remote location, but in the Sheraton Centre, a huge hotel located at Fifty-second Street and Seventh Avenue, just a block from Times Square. Ann had long dreamed of being able to take a trip to New York, but raising her children had been a higher priority. Remembering my first trip as a wide-eyed eighth-grader, and then subsequent ones as a college student, I was anxious not only to relive those experiences and explore new ventures but also especially to watch Ann fulfill this dream. There is no city like it in the world.

The brochure for this New York Computer Expo touted, "The fascinating world of computers returns to New York City to provide 'hands on' opportunities to try new hardware and software from top manufacturers." The daily fee for attendance was ten dollars, for which "show registrants may attend hourly lectures each day at no cost." This sounded perfect for us—and our meager budget.

Previously Ann alluded to the fact that not long before our scheduled departure date, air traffic controllers nationwide had called a strike. There were delays all over the country. Our flights from Little Rock were no exception, and by the time we arrived at the hotel it was in the wee hours of the morning. Red-eyed and exhausted, we found the hotel and approached the night check-in clerk.

"I'm sorry, but we were not able to hold your room." What? We had guaranteed it with our credit card! (Of course, since the new corporate bank account contained almost no money, we had booked the cheapest room they had.) Visions of sleeping in the lobby or trying to find another room at this time in the morning flashed through our minds.

"However, if you don't mind, we can offer you the large suite on the fiftieth floor."

Ann, always keeping an eye on our financial situation, asked, "How much more will that cost us?"

"Oh, no. It will be the same price."

A penthouse suite! For the same price?! We really were dreaming!

Unbelievable: a huge living room with not only a television and several chairs and sofas, but also an entertainment area with a wet bar and refrigerator. Then another television in the large bedroom. We could have invited ten friends to stay with us and not be crowded. The best part of all, though, was the view. Down fifty stories at our feet was Times Square, then on beyond, the East River. We could look out over many of the skyscrapers and down on microcosms of life in the windows and on the rooftops of this majestic city. I remember Ann's words, "Susan, this is all beautiful, but do you realize that there is only one way that we can go? Down?" She was not being pessimistic but was rather just mesmerized by the entire experience.

It was pure luck (or did God also have a hand in this penthouse arrangement?) that we had gotten this suite with this view instead of a tiny, crowded but sufficient room for our stay. A bonus was the fact that my brother and his oarsman son were in town for a rowing competition to be held nearby. How pleased we were to be able to share our good fortune with them. Looking down onto Times Square, my brother said, "Now this is the way that I like to experience New York!"

Yes, we were truly lucky with this arrangement and fortunate to get tickets for *Woman of the Year*. However, we did have a very serious mission for this trip. It was up to us to take this opportunity to learn all that we could to push our business forward and to take it to the next level. *Inspiration* had come from the Broadway play, then concrete, useful, factual *information* from the conference. To our credit, we did attend ten of the twenty-three available lectures— within the span of just a couple of days. That was rather impressive. Notes taken at the time are still filed in the folder "New York Computer Expo—August 12–15, 1981" and now reveal what true neophytes we were.

In one session, "Introduction to Small Business Systems," I recorded that "UNEX [sic] [is the] OS [operating system] of the future." At that point I didn't even know enough to spell UNIX correctly. It was ironic that within a few years our company would be a local authority and major supplier of computers powered by the UNIX operating system. We had a lot to learn.

One presenter, in discussing computer printers in the business environment, pointed out the differences in quality of the various models of dot matrix printers and recommended the "EBSON" [sic] as his favorite. As will be shown in subsequent chapters, Epson printers and computers played a significant role in our professional history.

One note taken during one of the seminar sessions has stayed not only in our files but also in our memories since that time. A single sentence spoken there has proven to be most profound in describing the computer industry from that day until this:

"There are two kinds of computers: experimental and obsolete."

In the years to follow, we would try to provide our clients with the very latest and most powerful computer technology only to discover often that it had not been developed and perfected to the degree that it had been purported to us. On the other hand, it became a fact of the industry that as soon as "the latest technology" was purchased and installed, immediately something faster, cheaper, and with greater storage capacity would be available. Experimental and obsolete.

The information we received at the New York conference was significant. We knew more about printers, disks, memory, COBOL, Pascal, CPUs and operating systems than when we had left. However, this knowledge was infinitesimal in relation to what we needed and would acquire in the future. The important point here is that we realized not only that we did need to learn more about computers, but also that we really did need to go ahead and purchase a computer of our own. No amount of study could compensate for the experience we would receive on the keyboard. So, what to buy?

Research had taught us that there was a wide chasm between the huge (literally) mainframe computers and the few smaller ones, the minicomputers, which were available for small businesses and a few homes. Among the few companies offering the latter was one that was started by two fellows working in a (you guessed it!) garage. They had succeeded in building a rather small (compared to the mainframes) computer, and decided to put it into production. When trying to decide on a name, they first came up with (I kid you not) "Kentucky Fried Computers." After a few months, however, they decided that that really didn't sound sufficiently professional. They changed their name to North Star Computers and moved their operations from the garage to an office complex in San Leandro, California, near San Francisco.

It didn't take very long for Ann and me to exhaust our possibilities. There were not many types of computers, and even fewer were within our price range. North Star kept making it to the shorter list, which had started out as not very long in the first place. Ultimately, we decided that this was the computer for us. Since there were only two or three stores in town that carried any computer-related products and only one with North Star, the choice of vendor was a simple matter: Computerland, located in the same shopping strip that in the future would house the very first TCBY store (useless but interesting trivia).

The memory of August 16, 1981, is vivid to this day. I was thrilled to carry our North Star Horizon to the car and gently nestle it into the blanket padding in the trunk. For a sense of perspective it should be pointed out that this machine must have been at least two feet wide, more than two feet deep and at least eight inches high. And that was just the *wooden* (yes, wooden) box that housed the processor, the memory, and the two 5¼-inch floppy disk drives. (These were the days when floppy disks really were floppy.) The bulky screen and keyboard were separate. Then the printer: mammoth! How proud and pleased we were. We were on our way! To where?

The computer was ours. It was then like a newborn baby just home from the hospital; now what were we going to do with it? I proudly set it onto a folding table in the little bedroom I had turned into my study. Cables and cords were connected. It was ready, but was I, were we? No.

At least we had already planned further study, the first session to take place the following weekend. Ann and I piled my daughter and her son into the car for an educational visit to Harrison, Arkansas. Since they were both still young, we entreated Ann's teenage daughter to accompany us and look after the little ones while we learned. Another interesting experience. Our instructor's living room was truly wall-to-wall computer equipment. There are two four-letter words, both beginning with "G," used to describe a person who is deeply involved in computers and programming: "geek" and "guru." Often one person is identified as both. Suffice it to say, Ann and I were thankful that this man was willing to give of his weekend time to help teach us much more about the features and possible future of our North Star.

About six weeks later, still struck with the vision of writing the next definitive medical computer system, I traveled to Ft. Worth for a comprehensive meeting entitled "Choosing and Using a Computer in a Private Medical Practice." Even though it was primarily aimed at the physicians in attendance, this course provided information to me that would be used in a manner quite different from that initially imagined. Upon arrival I was impressed that the hotel was the one where Jack and Jackie Kennedy had stayed before his fateful trip to Dallas. In contrast, I will admit that it was at this time that I first learned what it means to "assume" something, as the speaker broke that one word into three. Truly, though, over and above that, there was a great deal of substance in the lectures themselves, and, looking back over these notes now some twenty years later, I realize how much I did absorb during that trip.

It was a tribute to my own idealism and a blow to my sense of reality that I thought we really could, within a short period of time, write software that would automate offices of both small businesses and physicians' clinics. What a great idea it was—but what a bad idea it was! It didn't take us long at all to realize that the process of taking this project from drawing board to market would take a long time and many, many dollars. So, we looked further.

At that time, the small computer operating system du jour was CP/M (Control Program for Microcomputers), the one used by North Star for their systems. By the time we realized the folly of my idea to develop the previously mentioned programs, this company fortunately had developed a set of general accounting programs for small businesses. Software was available, ready to be sold and installed.

Again, a milestone. In the years to follow when Ann and I were questioned about reasons for our success, one answer would be a single word, "flexibility." This first change of plans, from being a software developer to a software reseller, was one that we had not anticipated. However, as the reality of the situation became apparent to us, we first accepted and then embraced the shift. In this case, it was wise for us to take the road more traveled.

By then we could no longer deny the fact that it truly was time to have some money coming *into* the company so that it could begin to balance the money going out. Ann and I were blessed to be receiving some widow's benefits from Social Security, but this money was to keep our households running, not to finance a growing company.

Once again the word "flexibility" popped up. Our North Star goals and plans were still being developed, but unexpectedly we heard of another, very different computer product, this one made by Texas Instruments: the TI 99/4A. In contrast to our huge (in desktop terms) North Star, the TI was so little. It even had a tiny keyboard. For viewing, it was hooked up to a television. There were a few basic but very useful modules available for it, even games. Best of all, it was inexpensive, easy to use, and would appeal to a vast array of consumers. A natural for us to sell, even to our friends and acquaintances.

Ann's marketing background kicked into gear as she taught me about the advantages of an attractive, informative folder with pictures, features, and benefits of the product. We first invited friends to our houses to see the TI. Then some friends allowed us to bring our "road show" to their homes and present the product to other groups of people, in presentations not unlike Tupperware parties. We even provided refreshments.

The immediate, hoped-for stampede did not occur, but God did provide hope in the son of a long-time friend of my family. This person, to whom we will be eternally grateful, actually bought a TI 99/4A from us, just before the end of our first fiscal year. Thus at end-of-year number one, we were able to report revenues (gross, not net) of $525.00. That is no misprint: five hundred twenty-five dollars. One should not laugh; we were thrilled!

That lowly figure did provide us several important insights:

- At least it was not zero.
- We were still quite green in the field of marketing.
- We had cut our teeth and were ready for the next course.

Then the trampoline!

"BREAK A LEG!"

Ann speaks:

In theatrical circles the phrase "Break a leg!" is often voiced to wish a performer good luck at the beginning of a show. Our previous attempts had been restricted to the ministry of THEOS and had placed us on a focused path to complete projects. Even so, Susan and I found ourselves wandering. We were going to need some real luck to formulate business plans that would prove to be profitable, as we were not yet on a steady and chartered course.

Yes, the New York trip had provided a basis for us to start thinking about business and industry trends. We started to increase our knowledge not only of computers but also of business. Whatever work we accomplished in one or the other of the "offices" we had in our homes was constantly interrupted, however. Our children, yard work, housework, and personal business provided easy distractions from the business at hand.

Then something happened that provided a reality check. I was exercising on a small trampoline in my den because the weather was cold and ice was beginning to form on the streets. I distinctly remember coming down on the side of the trampoline and hearing, as well as feeling, a loud pop. No, it wasn't my leg; it was my ankle that broke. I knew in an instant that it was serious, and I lay clumsily on my den floor until I was able to use the telephone. How could I have been so stupid? This accident was going to force me to curtail drastically many activities, and how was I going to take care of my household chores in this condition?

My first reaction was to call Susan. I told her what had happened, that I was in excruciating pain, and that I could already feel the ankle beginning to swell. I asked her to please come help me. The streets were slick and icy, but I had no other choice. I knew I had broken my ankle, and it needed to be set immediately and put into a cast.

Susan and I have discovered over the years that regardless of the time, day or night, if one of us needs anything, the other responds immediately. Neither of us having a man in the house, we came to depend on each other in a variety of situations, including the births of kittens and puppies. Our children were as helpful as possible, but we did have to remind ourselves that they were, indeed, children, and that there were times when only another adult could or should be depended upon. This was one of those times. Susan assured me that she would be there as quickly as she could.

Under normal conditions it would take only about twelve minutes to get from Susan's house to mine, but that day conditions were far from normal. The roads were icy—really icy. Finally, about an hour after leaving, Susan arrived to find me in a helpless condition. I had really done a number on my ankle, and the pain had become quite intense. My ankle was more purple and more swollen than when I had called Susan, and I knew I needed to get to the orthopedic clinic very soon. Fortunately, she had called the clinic, and the doctor was expecting my arrival.

Once again, Susan ventured onto the hazardous road, and slight rises were obstacles to maneuver and conquer. After what seemed like an inordinate amount of time, we arrived at the front door of the clinic. There was only a skeleton staff, and a nurse finally rolled out a wheelchair for me. I was immediately wheeled to a patient room and helped onto a table for the doctor to examine my injury. When I looked up, who should appear at the door but the same doctor who had done the Herrington Rod procedure on my husband's spine just a few months before? I was unable to see the spiritual application due to my intense pain. It was evident though, that the doctor had a great deal of compassion for me because of my recent tragedy, and he took all precautions to properly diagnose my injury. He was also very delicate in not making fun of my calamity. I have heard that doctors will sometimes tease patients when they have suffered a ridiculous accident, and I thought it was never helpful to the patient. This was no joking matter to me; I hurt enough to bite a bullet and even wished one was provided. By then, my ankle was twice its normal size.

After a series of X-rays, a cast was fitted to my ankle and I was given crutches. Once again, the icy roads were our enemy as we proceeded back home to get me settled and comfortable. Fortunately, the doctor provided a few pain pills, which helped until I was able to get a prescription filled once the weather had improved. All I could think about was getting home and going to bed. I had always been active in sports, and I had broken a number of bones due to my activity. I was even accused of being clumsy, and I have to agree that this was probably the case. I had experienced the pain of broken bones before, but I have to say that this injury was by far the most painful break I had experienced.

In addition to my physical pain, the problem of how I was going to maintain my household was really bearing down on me. How was I going to take care of my family? My sons were still living at home, and there were meals to cook and laundry to be done. After some discussion, it was mutually decided that Susan and her daughter would move into my house for a brief period until I was able to get a handle on my pain and could maneuver my crutches. For about ten days, I was only able to sleep with the aid of pain pills. I had a lot of time to try to sort out the lesson to be learned from this experience. It is amazing how God will sometimes place us on our backs in order to put us in a mode of thinking that we would not normally engage in when our lives are busy and filled with activity. I had six weeks to think about plans for our business.

We decided to bring the computer to my house and set it up on a folding table in my bedroom. This was done as a convenience to me since I was still on crutches. While the children were at school or playing out in the yard, we worked not only on the computer but also on more definite plans for the direction of our business. Although it now seems so humble, even quaint, this was a tremendously important step in the future of our company. We were in the same room for hours at a time, finally really working on the business and its formation.

For reasons that made perfect sense at the time, we decided it would be best for me to go to California to attend the training sessions required for resellers. By then, my ankle had healed to the point that I no longer needed crutches but wore a bulky boot. I was determined to go now that I was back on my feet!

Some people in life are natural-born navigators. I am not one of these people. I was an inexperienced traveler, and I was used to letting my husband look for directions while driving. I found myself on a plane traveling to a strange city without the slightest idea how to get to the workshop when I arrived. All I had in my hand was a map provided by a travel agent and a confirmation that I had booked a rental car. I vividly remember spending most of the time from Dallas to my final destination studying every aspect of the map and trying to convince myself I had the confidence to get there. There was no way that I was going to get lost; I simply decided that it would not happen. Persistence and determination were all I possessed at that time. Confidence would have to come later.

Finally, I arrived at my destination, only to find that the motel where I was staying was located in a really rough section of town. I was afraid to go out of my room after dark, so I didn't. The light of day offers much more confidence to a scared traveler who is unsure of her destination. I was able to use the map and get to the headquarters the next morning after my arrival, and I found the building where the training classes were being held. After all, no one had to know the scary and unusual experiences I had encountered getting there.

Attending the training sessions was a real eye-opener. The room was filled with knowledgeable people who all seemed to be computer gurus. They even talked in a language that I was not used to hearing. Some people have referred to this as "computerese." I kept my ears open and my mouth shut most of the time. As I always do when attending a seminar, I took lots of notes. I needed these to refer to later. I was able to focus on the marketing part of the session because I had majored in marketing in college and because my husband and stepfather had both been salesmen. Marketing a product came easily to me, and I loved the process. To me, marketing is like being an artist who paints a picture and sells it. It is the process of completing the sale and putting a bow on it that gives me the rush. After the sessions were over, I came home with a new confidence in my ability to help forge a successful business.

Previously, we had become a reseller for a Texas Instruments product geared for home use and for educational institutions. This product was called the TI 99/4A. It was a very innovative product and light years ahead of its time. The product came with a lot of educational software, which was appealing to local schools. We were flooded with requests for demos. But in spite of the apparent interest, we found that educational institution sales were difficult because of the purchasing red tape involved. However, the time we spent proved to be a training ground for us and gave us wonderful experience and exposure to the public.

During all this time, we continued to devote much time to THEOS. In April of 1982, we helped establish a second chapter in Pine Bluff, Arkansas. By now the word was spreading about this wonderful ministry, and people who had been driving from Pine Bluff to the Little Rock meetings now had their own chapter. The Little Rock chapter continued to thrive and grow in numbers. People in other parts of the state wanted us to help establish and organize additional chapters. We felt torn much of the time because we did not want to neglect THEOS, and yet we could see opportunities opening up for our business. It was as though the THEOS ministry was the catalyst for our business, and we thought of our business as an extension of this ministry. Although our husbands were deceased, we felt their presence in everything we did, and they seemed to be cheering us on and helping us along the way.

Not long after our many demos with the TI product, we realized that we were going to need to move into a professional office in order to conduct business. After all, we couldn't say, "Come to our home and we will show you our computer." Business is not conducted this way. We also felt that being in a professional setting would make us feel more professional. In order to move, we needed to go to a banker and establish a credit line for "seed" money to operate. This was another big step in our business career, and it would bring some unexpected fringe benefits.

We felt so professional the day we went to the main office of one of the largest banks in Little Rock. (Once again there was irony in the fact that Susan and I were using the same bank during each of our estate-settlement activities.) I still think back with gratitude as I picture the kind face of the banker who was in charge of the Commercial Loan Department. He did not scoff at our idea, nor did he laugh (while we were there, anyway) at the small sum we were requesting. It was evident in our words and demeanor that ten thousand dollars seemed like a huge amount to request, especially when we had nothing but an idea to back it. No, I am not kidding myself, we did have to sign personal guarantees, but the important factor was that at that point another person was exhibiting confidence in us and in our ideas. This confidence spurred us on to begin to take ourselves more seriously.

Our visit to the banker brought a revelation that would be important in our business as well as in the relationship with our banker: we both had untarnished reputations within the financial community. No loans, interest or principal, had gone unpaid; no bills were past due; there was absolutely no hint of poor money management in our history. It was unspoken and assumed on that day, but it was up to us to maintain a record of fiscal honesty and trustworthiness. We had already formed a bond of trust between each other through our friendship, and now we expanded that trust to our finances. I can't stress enough the importance of being able to trust a business partner. Through all of the good and bad times we experienced in the nineteen years in business and the worries that were a natural part of this, trust was never an issue. I believe to this day that trust was a key factor in our ability to hold our business together through thick and thin.

Looking back on everything, I realize now that breaking my ankle was the best thing that could have happened. It indeed gave us the "push in the right direction." When trials come, if we have faith that we are being molded, tested, and prepared for the next stage of life, we can see the blessing of adversity. Suffering can provide great opportunities for us to do the things we have only imagined for ourselves.

At that point, Susan and I had no idea of the successes that would come in the ensuing years, but we acted like there was no possible way that we were going to fail. This is an important key to our success. We wanted to be successful, so we acted as if we were successful. At that point, we had mentally set a goal to work toward, and the mind always finds a way to try and achieve the goal.

ON OUR WAY!

Susan speaks:

"Nae man can tether Time or Tide," penned Robert Burns in his work *Tam O'Shanter.* We two women were certainly unable to "tether Time." Even though it did seem to stand still briefly with Ann's accident, it kept urging us to keep going, keep going, keep going. "The Little Engine that Could" Syndrome was taking hold of our lives and our energies. We thought we could; we thought we could—but it was still all uphill.

Once Ann became more mobile, we moved the computer and our books down to her family room. Fortunately it was rather large, as it soon doubled as a demo/marketing area for the first few prospects that we had. Since the one sale we had made was to a very close family friend, he was most willing to come to her house to pick up the purchase on his way from Arkadelphia to Little Rock, and we did not feel uncomfortable at all about asking him to do so.

However, if indeed we were going to remain true to our mission, if we really were going to step up the professionalism of our company and the size of the systems to sell, we needed to take our next leap of faith: renting office space. This sounds like such a basic, logical procedure. Of course a business needs an office. However, with a still almost non-existent revenue stream, this was a very big deal to us. This was a commitment, not a one-time "here is the money; now I'll take the computer" type of transaction. There would be rent due each and every month. Besides, it wasn't just the office we had to

consider, but also the desks, and the bookcases, and the other furnishings, and the utilities, and the telephone, and the receptionist and
the insurance, and the...and the...and the.... How many rooms would
we need? Offices, yes, but also a waiting/reception room and at least
one bathroom. Such a seemingly simple thing isn't.

Our search began: yellow pages, classified ads, telephone calls.
After extensive investigation of the available offices and gasps at the
prices being asked, we finally came upon a description that sounded
very interesting. Our quest had initially focused on spaces that were
nothing more than that, just empty rooms. Then we found an advertisement for a novel arrangement, a co-operative office environment.
Intriguing...definitely worth further inquiry.

This #2 Financial Centre was easy to find since it was one of
few buildings on the newly constructed Financial Parkway just west
of, and perpendicular to, Shackleford Road. This area of Little Rock
had certainly changed. Six short years prior to that, Financial Parkway had not even existed. How well I remember early 1975, being
in the final trimester of pregnancy! We knew that our baby was to
be born at Baptist Hospital and also that the shortest distance between our house and the Baptist was via this same section of
Shackleford Road. Several weeks before the due date I traveled that
road, trying to picture what it would be like being in labor and having to drive (or, hopefully, being driven) on it. Hilly! Up and down
and up and down. Potholes! There were so many that it was almost
impossible to miss all of them. It was a matter of aiming for the smallest ones. Such a vision: hilly and bouncy and me in labor!

By the year 1981, my daughter was a healthy five-and-a-half-year-
old source of untold joy. The Shackleford Road hills had been leveled,
the quaint little homes of German families had been moved or torn
down, and the two lanes were expanded to four (with no potholes).
Financial Parkway had been built, extending but a couple of miles
west at that time, and both #1 and #2 Financial Centre office buildings had been constructed. At that time this location was on the western outskirts of Little Rock's business and financial community,
although it now almost seems like a part of downtown since the city
has continued its steady march in that direction.

Driving up to the front entrance, we were immediately impressed by the name, "Centre" not "Center"; that was classy. A flashback: wasn't that New York Computer Expo held at the Sheraton *Centre*? (Probably more irrelevant trivia.) The ad said this office was on the top floor.

We pressed "4" on the elevator control panel. There was a slight shudder as the mechanisms took hold and initiated our ascent. Ding—second floor; ding—third floor. We both had mixed feelings of excited expectancy slightly shrouded with apprehension. Just like the heavy velvet curtains at the Palace Theater, the elevator door stayed closed, a barrier between us and whatever was to be revealed to us when it opened. The final ding—open it did. Stepping out, we entered a large central room, furnished with several sofas, chairs, and tables, and also a huge receptionist's desk.

Immediately, we were greeted warmly by the perky, friendly receptionist, so tiny that she was dwarfed by the desk. She asked about our needs and then offered a tour of the facility. The entire area was one large suite of offices. From the interior reception room there were doors leading into the continuous hall that went all the way around the suite, forming a huge rectangle. There were offices on the left and offices on the right. Since the suite was, indeed, rectangular, this meant that most of the offices on one side of the hall had lovely views of the city; the others had no view because they had no windows. Undoubtedly, the rent rates would be partially determined by the view.

As the tour progressed, it became evident that this young lady was much more than just a receptionist; her marketing acumen bubbled to the surface as she began describing the features and benefits of leasing space in this very suite. "You see, you have a choice. If you want to answer your own calls, you may do so. However, when you are in conference or away from the office, let me know, and I will answer your calls here at the switchboard." *Telephones! A receptionist!*

"Anyone who is waiting to see you will be able to sit there, in the main waiting room, and the bathrooms and water fountains are down the hall." *Waiting room! Bathrooms! The water fountains were a bonus that we had not even considered.*

"Now this is the office space that you might like. I know that it has no windows and is only one room, but note that there are two built-in desks with bookcases above." *Desks! Bookcases!*

"The monthly fee I quoted includes all we have discussed, along with the utilities." *Utilities!*

Amazingly, this figure was within our reach. We could not believe that the one fee included almost all the details that had worried us. This was our first first-hand corporate example of the "economy of scale," the "economy of shared resources," and a *lagniappe* from God. Yes, He had once again provided, even down to the built-in bookcases. However, He had also thrown in that bonus that we had not even considered: the water fountains!

After signing the lease papers, all we had to do was to buy two desk chairs, a brown fold-up table for the computer—and, most importantly—a coffee pot. No windows, so no need to buy shades or curtains. Even with the computer, we owned so little of value that insurance was not even needed. All in all, our expenses were minimal. We were set. We were ready!

Within this time period, we had been very thankful for the TI sales that continued to roll into our coffers. However, the proverbial handwriting was on the wall. The TI 99/4A was becoming a readily available commodity, sold at low margins by entities much larger than Custom Software Consultants. What a sinking feeling to open the Arkansas Gazette and be confronted with the huge ad from the city's largest department store. Even they are selling them? In addition, several groups began marketing the TI in pyramid sales programs. Once again the "F" word (flexibility) came into play; the game plan had to change as the TI faded from our scope.

Fortunately, concurrently, the development of our North Star line was advancing. The general accounting software that had been developed and marketed by them was proving to be versatile and dependable. A business could choose whether to use only one or a number of the programs, including the General Ledger, Accounts Payable, Accounts Receivable, Payroll, and such. Each could stand alone as a separate product or could integrate with the others to form a

complete accounting system. We realized that it was time for me
to go to San Leandro and receive further training from North Star
on these programs. (I was in San Francisco recently, visiting my
daughter and her husband. Traveling on the BART—Bay Area Rapid
Transit—between The City and Hayward we slowed at one station,
then stopped for passenger interchange. The station sign read "San
Leandro." Could it really have been almost twenty years since my first
trip there? But I digress.)

Thank Heavens (honestly!) the accounting software was truly as
versatile as claimed. A review of our first clients is almost comical.
What a variety of business types! Such diversity! Real estate, farm-
ing, public accounting, formal wear rental, insurance, property management, oil distribution, and even a waste management company. We
neither discriminated nor verticalized. A sale was a sale was a sale,
and we needed the sales. Needless to say, our professional lives were
far from boring!

By this time North Star had announced a companion product
to the Horizon line—the North Star Advantage. What an innovative
concept to house all components in one case, except the printer of
course! There in one compact unit were the screen, the keyboard,
and the two 5¼-disk drives, with all necessary components, including the processor, power supply, and various controllers tucked neatly
inside. Our product line was greatly expanded with this offering, since
the Advantage provided an alternative for the client. He or she had a
choice between the Horizon with separate components and the all-
in-one Advantage. Furthermore, the Advantage could be ordered in
three different sizes, well, storage capacities, to be exact. The disk
drives were still the 5¼-floppy type, but the computer could be con-
figured with either two floppy drives, one floppy and one *five megabyte* (no, that is not a misprint, that is *mega*) hard disk, or one floppy
and one *fifteen megabyte* hard disk. We could not even imagine how
anyone would need anything that would hold as much data as a fifteen megabyte drive would provide. It seemed the entire city could
be run with a drive that large. I well remember a farmer client who
at first ordered the smaller hard drive then changed his mind and
switched to the double floppy, thinking that the former would be

more than he would ever require for his system.

"Ann, some day we are going to look back on this and laugh." At that moment, though, neither of us was amused. In formal business suits, complete with high heels, we were walking from our parked car along the then-pedestrian-mall portion of Main Street toward the offices of a property management company prospect, carrying an Advantage in our (my) arms. Now this all-in-one concept is quite clever, except when one considers the fact that carrying all of it in one is not so much fun. Undoubtedly, Ann was just as burdened with the books and brochures that were part of our usual demo and sales pitch. It is amazing how much worse toes can hurt when the discomfort produced by high heels is exacerbated by the additional weight of a computer. (At that time the purchase of an equipment cart was not in our budget.) The combination brick and concrete sidewalk did not help, either. Finally, our destination. I was especially thankful for the few moments of relief provided by handrails inside the elevator.

Often pain and endurance were rewarded. The prospect became a client and not only remained loyal to our products for a number of years but also served as an excellent reference site as well. We were doing whatever needed to be done to help our business succeed. If that meant carrying a computer system down Main Street Mall, that was fine; we did it.

Before leaving the description of the Advantage, I need to mention one more of its features that would become important in the unfolding history of the computer industry. Since its introduction in 1975 and then further development in 1977, the CP/M (Computer Program for Microcomputers) operating system had been used by many, perhaps most, of the smaller computers. By 1981 and 1982 another, DOS (Disk Operating System), was made available. How innovative of North Star to enable the Advantage to function as *either* a CP/M or a DOS machine! This newer operating system got quite a boost when a version of it was introduced and promoted as MS-DOS, or Microsoft DOS. North Star had its eyes on the future.

Another historical note is that during this same time frame another company, Osborne, released the first successful CP/M portable business computer. Portable? Yes. Convenient? No—since the case for this "portable" device approximated the size and shape of a small sewing machine. Innovative but so unwieldy! What a kinship I feel to the Osborne as I generate this document on one of its descendants, my new, light 700 MHz, Pentium III laptop, which is loaded with a 20Gb hard drive, 128Mb memory, CD/DVD drive, USB port and so on and so on—and measures a mere 1.5"x13"x10". All within my lifetime!

Even though a lot of our business activity was comprised of general accounting system demos and sales, we had not forgotten the medical world. By this time more and more software was available for the CP/M computers, and, of course, that included our North Stars, both the Horizon and the Advantage. Fortunately, after researching the industry, Ann and I were able to find a system designed specifically for the management of medical offices. This was the fulfillment of a dream of mine, once I admitted the folly of writing my own.

As previously mentioned, while working as an orthopedic clinic office manager during Frank's residency, I was involved with the purchase of a computer system for that office. Then, very few clinics had systems. Ours was even more inventive than others since there was but one system being shared by two offices. The computer was housed at another orthopedic clinic (ironically, the one that Frank would join a few years hence), but we at our site stored and accessed information via telephone lines. If it were possible to revisit that system today, we would undoubtedly wonder how we were able to function at those transmission speeds, or lack thereof. We did because it didn't even dawn on us that it should or could be faster than that. Also, we were so thankful we had a printer that would fill out the required information onto the insurance forms. We no longer had to do them by hand!

Having enjoyed working on that system, I was thrilled that our own company was then able to offer a similar, and undoubtedly much better, one to our clients. It was a good system, one that we were ready to market full tilt. The no-turning-back point came when we rented a booth at the 1982 Arkansas Medical Society Meeting in Hot Springs. We were telling the state's medical community that we were committed to this market and were ready to move forward. This was a good move, since we were able to meet many doctors at the meeting. Afterwards, we started to receive calls of inquiry. People were actually calling us!

We really started feeling good about this product when a reputable physicians' management consultant called and wanted to come talk with us about it and see a demo. Our little office still had no windows, and the desks were still built-in, but we were proud of it. Before the consultant arrived, I went to school to retrieve my daughter and brought her to the office, where she started playing around, barefoot as usual. A splinter, almost invisible to the eye, can cause great pain to the foot of a seven-year-old. Before I could tend to the problem, the consultant arrived. A parent himself, he kindly offered to perform a "splinterectomy."

Penn asked tearfully, "Are you a doctor?"

"No, but I am close enough!"

He was, and performed the procedure delicately but successfully. He later recommended our products and services to a number of his clients. His caring ways spilled over into his professional life. I remember hearing him talking a couple of years later about one of our clients-in-common. "Every time I think of him, I want to pop my buttons with pride. He came from such a meager background and is doing so very well!" We wanted to continue to work with people such as these—those who succeeded despite initial odds and those who recognized and applauded the achievements of others.

It was a real testimony to our friendship that Ann and I could co-exist in that one little windowless office for as long as we did. As indicated before, our personalities and strengths are complementary. However, complementary still means different, and "differents" can get on each other's nerves after a while. Fortunately (how often that word is appearing), the office directly across the hall became available. The bad news was that it had no built-ins and was quite a bit smaller than the first room; however, the good news: *windows*. We were able to purchase the tiny (elegant but not practical!) desks and credenzas from the former occupants—and spread out. Besides, we felt that it was quite impressive to have a "room with a view" in which to demo our systems and to talk with prospective clients.

More and more doctors became interested in our products, but we still did not lose sight of our bread-and-butter general accounting systems. Then came another interesting twist in the form of agricultural systems. This one was completely unexpected, but welcome, since the revenues from the medical segment had not really begun. We started meeting with a man from Hot Springs who had designed a system that provided many of the computing functions needed not only by farmers but also ancillary agricultural support businesses, such as equipment suppliers. There was no indication where this might lead.

By the end of 1982, Custom Software Consultants had developed a favorable and significant reputation within the North Star Company and had become acquainted with many of its employees through our trips to San Leandro and innumerable telephone conversations. One of these employees mentioned to us another computer show, COMDEX. We had never heard of it. They said they hoped we could attend since North Star would have a booth and many of their people would be there.

"Where will it be?" Las Vegas! Great place to visit. I had been there twice before. The first time was during a cross-country drive with my husband, arriving the very next day after we had hiked not only *down into* the Grand Canyon but also *back up* to the rim on the same day! This is not to be recommended to anyone, and we had almost set our sights dangerously high. However, by the time we arrived in Las Vegas, we had recuperated somewhat, except for the huge blisters on most of our toes. Even those did not prevent our enjoying the city and its non-stop activities. The second time was a brief overnight refueling stop in a small plane as part of a trip between Little Rock and San Francisco. I was ready for a return visit.

Ann and I decided that with the reasonable airfares and even more inexpensive accommodations, meals, and entertainment, we would try it this once. COMDEX, that did sound interesting!

It was—and such a contrast to that first New York Computer Expo. This was a huge convention! How inexperienced we felt as we stood in a long, long line just to register. Resisting the temptation to let out a loud "mooooooo," we crept along in the well-ordered line that wove back and forth and back and forth until finally we reached the desk where we were handed our badges. Just beyond, through the doors, was the Great Hall of the Las Vegas Convention Center. Thousands of people and hundreds of booths. At first we felt lost and overwhelmed.

How welcome the sight of the distinctive navy blue star above North Star's booth! Familiar faces! At least feeling welcome with this group gave us confidence to proceed through the rest of the week. Confidence we had, but rested feet, no. These were the days when everyone, except the real hippie-type programmers, wore complete business attire to these conventions. Here we were once again in conservative suits and, yes, high heel shoes. The entire floor of the convention center is one continuous slab of concrete. Although the planners were mindful of that and laid thin carpeting along the aisles between exhibits, there was little relief. Soon, we began feigning interest in certain products for long periods of time just because their booths had either comfortable chairs or thick carpeting, or both.

By noon of the second day, we came upon a plan. "You wear size ten shoes, don't you? I wear size ten also. Why don't we switch shoes for a little while?" Brilliant. It is amazing how much relief can be had from shoes that apply pressure in slightly different places. I am still not sure whether that meant that by the end of the day our feet were more relieved by this tactic or whether they were so sore *all over* that they were completely numb.

That was our first of many COMDEX shows.

SALES COME ROLLING IN

8

Ann speaks:

When Susan and I attended the COMDEX convention in the latter part of 1982, we had no idea how much of a change this would make in our current business strategies.

Computers were beginning to "catch on" because they had become "micro" in nature and were quickly becoming a household buzzword in the minds of consumers. We saw many early entries into the personal computer marketplace, but one product especially caught our interest. It was the Epson QX-10 computer that came equipped with a Valdocs word processing package that ran under the CP/M operating system. We were currently selling a business computer that ran under this same operating system, so it seemed logical that we also look at this product.

I do not know if it was coincidence or other factors that controlled our thinking processes at the time, but we seemed to be drawn naturally to having more than one product to market. It seemed reasonable that with two products at hand, our probability for success increased dramatically. We could market our present computer to business applications and then begin to move into the personal computer market which seemed to be quickly emerging. I had always been taught that the more fishing lines you have out there, the more you can reel in.

The Epson Company itself had been a front-runner in the marketplace for years with the presence of their many lines of printers.

The QX-10 was their first attempt to get into the computer arena. This product was able to bridge the gap to the average person with ease of use. Most people are not programmers, and the other current products demanded that one be somewhat computer literate to understand how to handle all of the instructions necessary to operate them. With the Epson QX-10, however, the average person who had never used a computer could sit down and, with just a small amount of instruction, start doing word processing and spreadsheet applications. That ability provided a real "breakthrough" to the public. It was a marvelous product, and we were determined to throw our entire selves into it and make it a winner. It has often been stated that the first person to introduce a new idea usually ends up being the leader of the pack. We were determined to take that slot and made plans to market this "baby" as soon as we could get our hands on it.

Upon our return from COMDEX, we put on our "other hat" and attended the Arkansas Cattlemen's Association Show, which was held in a downtown convention area. Our other computer line had a wonderful agricultural package that was geared to farmers. We demonstrated this product at our booth and made quite a hit with our boots that we wore to fit the persona of the audience. We actually sold quite a number of these agri-software packages to farmers by attending the Farm Equipment Show held in the spring of 1983, as well.

The next few weeks were filled with demos, demos, demos; first to farmers and then to accounting firms. We even sold a very comprehensive accounting package to a real estate company. We also had several physicians who were interested in computerizing their medical offices and managed to sell a couple of these packages. In the midst of all of this business activity, we helped launch another THEOS chapter, our third, in Benton. The interest in THEOS had continued to mount, and we were beginning to have difficulty managing all of our priorities and the business opportunities that were coming our way. After all, we were still mothers who were responsible for raising our children and were expected to wear a number of "hats" during this time. The roles of a single mother were demanding, especially when we were also trying to build our own business. Sometimes there weren't enough hours in the day to get everything done.

By this time our offices were becoming very cramped, and we could only deal with having one person for a demo. We inquired of the landlord and found that there was an office suite on the first floor that was available. We jumped at the opportunity and felt very prosperous and professional with our new office. It was the first office seen upon entrance to the building, and the back of it had a wonderful view of the atrium. We thought it was plenty of space for several years. When we moved, we hired our first employee to answer the phone and do administrative work. Nancy had been visiting our THEOS group because she was widowed. She had been married to a physician and had three children. It made us feel good to hire her because she was a very capable person and because we were helping a single mother support her family. This bond made for a very pleasant and rewarding relationship in our office.

As we began selling systems, our customers were interested in purchasing service contracts for their hardware. We had tried to subcontract most of this work, but the number of systems we were selling created a real need to get our own in-house service technician and the need for a second employee. Of course, the technician would have to be sent to North Star in California to be trained as a certified technician. In our inexperience, we didn't realize that a credit card was needed to rent a car, and our new technician had quite a time on his California trip. We assumed he had his own credit card, but they were asking for a "company" credit card. Of course we didn't have one, but managed to wire the money to them and the hotel where he was staying. We made a note to apply for a company credit card the very next week so that we wouldn't have another episode of this nature.

Again, there was another COMDEX show held in the spring that we needed to attend, this time in Atlanta. There was another purpose in attending this show, and that was to become certified and authorized to sell our "dream" product, the Epson computer. Until we made an effort to become certified, we could not launch this new product that we were dying to put into our sales mix. As you might expect, we did both attend the conference and came back with our official "certification" that entitled us to press full steam ahead in marketing the new product.

Since the Epson computer was a consumer product, it was necessary for us to start advertising the product and use any available method to get the name before the public. Once we did this, interest for this product began to increase. So much interest developed that we found it necessary to hire another employee. She helped with proposals and administrative work until one day we discovered what a gifted salesperson she was. From that day forth, her days were filled with demos for interested prospects. I packaged the marketing programs and prospected the clients, and she demonstrated the computer.

In the beginning, the only software we had to sell was the basic package that came with the computer. As sales became commonplace, people began asking us to find other software that would also run on the computer, and we spent a great deal of time engaging in this process. Pretty soon, we became known as the "experts" for the Epson product and our days became even busier. We were going everywhere to demo, not just offering demos in our office. We were now ordering many units at the same time because the company continued to offer lower prices for just a "few more" units ordered at the same time.

We continued to attend business shows and frequently had a booth all our own. We even exhibited at a Home Economics State Meeting and appeared at a booth at the Southern Living Cooking Show. Everywhere we went, we would take our official "salesperson" with us; she would dazzle the interested individuals, and we could always count on a few sales emerging from her presence. Business increased so much that we decided to hire another female salesperson. After all, it worked the first time, why not try it again?

The exhilaration of success did not keep Susan and me from being tired at the end of a long day. I think it was our sense of humor that kept us from becoming totally exhausted. We were never too tired to laugh at ourselves, and our naive foray into the "man's world" of business provided us with a number of occasions to do just that. One such incident comes to mind from the summer of 1983. A grocery store that was interested in the product to computerize their operations called us and said, "Bring one to me." We thought they meant they wanted to buy the product when they actually meant they wanted to see the product. We drove several miles to deliver the computer, but they ended up not taking it. One of the lessons we learned while establishing a business is, "a deal is not a deal until the contract is signed."

We even had a lady buy a computer from us and then change her mind weeks after we had delivered the product. We spent countless hours trying to train her on it. Sometimes it is better to just say "ok" and give the customer her money back. All of these things have to be learned, and there is no possible way of escaping the experience of these mistakes that gives you the knowledge and wisdom that is needed to become a sophisticated business owner. I truly thank God for all of these lessons, because they helped to build character and to protect us from further lessons down the road which could have been much more costly in nature.

Believe it or not, we still kept up our North Star business, and Susan spent most of her time doing demos for this particular area of our business. Fortunately these demos were more planned in nature, and the sales life cycle was quite different from the retail product. Sometimes the sales conflicted because people also looked at the other product to fill their needs. We had to be very careful to properly market the right product with the right prospect. After all, the North Star was still a better business product and was manufactured with more software available for that purpose. Because sales were increasing, we decided to hire a technical person for the North Star and a salesperson who could help demo the product. By that time, Susan and I had become very busy handling all of the details of a growing and thriving business. We were up to seven employees including ourselves.

In August of that year, it was time to take my son to college for the very first time. Where had the time gone? His Dad had been dead for three years, so it was important for me to take a particular interest in accompanying him to the campus in Jonesboro. It was not only a very bleak day weather wise, but it was also a bleak experience to return without my son. Under normal circumstances it would have been an exciting day for a young man to journey to a new experience of making new friends and forming a new life. We both felt the tremendous void in our lives that day because of the absence of his dad, and I did all that was in my power to put forth a positive attitude. I did not want him to remember seeing his mother crying and sobbing as he walked to his dormitory. The tears flowed unashamedly on the drive back home, though. He confessed many years after this incident that he had also cried.

Surviving the death of a loved one teaches that no one can replace that person, and that one's life is never the same after the experience. We also had to deal with the circumstances surrounding Bill's death, which were far from ordinary. Yes, there was still a lot of healing that needed to take place and that is why I felt so strongly the need to keep up my work with the THEOS ministry. I knew how others felt and would continue to feel for many years to come. I was living proof of that theory.

After I returned from taking Brad to college, Susan and I realized that we were becoming more of a "retail" business and our location was not suited to that change in strategy. We had heard that a strip shopping mall was going to be built and would be ready in the first quarter of 1984. We met with the real estate company that managed the property where we were presently housed and decided the time had come to put in a bid for the retail space.

The area was particularly attractive because we had an opportunity to situate ourselves on the end of the strip mall, and this location had access to two streets of traffic. It has been said that the most important aspect of a business setting is location, location, location. There, we would be "noticed" by everyone who drove by. We hoped that our name would become a household name and that everyone would think of computers as they saw our new name "Computer Systems Integrators." We had started our business with the name of Custom Software Consultants but changed it because we no longer planned to write software. After observing traffic patterns in that section of the city and talking with city planners, we decided to move when the space was available. We could make do with our current business location until that time. We would simply squeeze more people and computers into our existing space.

The fall of 1983 brought our best quarter of business. We were selling several computers a week, and noticed that we naturally appealed more to the professional environment, such as physicians, attorneys, etc. We began advertising in the newspaper and building our hype that we were moving to a new location. In that location, we would have a large training room and would train everyone who bought a system from us. We would also be offering door prizes and specials to those who attended our grand opening.

The time came to attend another COMDEX show. We had no idea what experiences lay ahead of us.

GOALS AND GAMES

9

Susan speaks:

COMDEX to COMDEX to COMDEX. It seemed that the life of our business was measured not by remembering the anniversary date of its founding but by the events that happened during and between these mammoth conventions. Once again Mother was more than willing to stay with Penn while Ann and I flew to Las Vegas on November 29, 1983. A note on my calendar indicates that we stayed in the Sahara Hotel, at the rate of fifty-three dollars per night, for a double room.

Right on "The Strip," the Sahara was within a convenient walking distance to most of the activities and exhibits. Even though we did enjoy walking whenever we could, taxis became important during this visit.

Late one afternoon we returned to the hotel after a long day on the convention floor, kicked off our shoes, then spent more time than usual getting ready for the evening ahead. Finally, elegantly decked and coiffed, we stepped through the Sahara's front door, emerging under the luminous marquee emblazoned with glittering, yes, even glitzy, lights and mirrors. "Taxi, please!" Although our fancy shoes were far from comfortable, it was the desire to arrive with hairdos intact that prompted us to hail a cab for the short trip to another hotel. Even though this certainly was no limousine, Ann and I still felt like starlets as we pulled up to the Desert Inn, alighted from the vehicle, and strode into the elegance of this famous place.

Smaller and definitely more understated than its showy neighbors, the Desert Inn stood but a few stories high in the center and flowed into lower annexes, then finally toward an array of individual cottages. Just beyond lay the hotel's private golf course.

"The Epson party, please!" (See, by then, I had learned to spell it correctly!)

"Through these doors, outside, around the first swimming pool, then into the building opposite. Others will show you from there."

Although the room was full, we were greeted warmly and made to feel not only welcome but also important. By then, the two ladies from Little Rock had started to make an impact, perhaps also an imprint. People knew who we were.

"Susan, have you *ever* seen shrimp this size? Maybe just one more...plateful, that is!"

"Look at that ice sculpture...oh, I mean, *those* ice sculptures!"

This spread was the embodiment of the phrase "lavish extravagance." Not only were the shrimp enormous and the ice sculptures dramatic, but also the sheer volume of food in that room was astounding. We could say honestly that neither of us had ever before attended a party for which sushi makers had been flown in from Tokyo. Yes, we were impressed, tremendously impressed. However, we both tried very hard to maintain a modestly aloof decorum. No one should be given reason to think that just because we were from Arkansas we hadn't been exposed to events such as this before.

Despite the magnificence of the occasion, its significance transcended the few hours at the Desert Inn. "Ann, do you realize that we are here, at this incredible party, not because of what our husbands accomplished, but rather because of what you and I have done?" No disrespect was intended. Our marriages had both ended through circumstances completely beyond our control. Those chapters of our lives were closed. We had survived, but being at this party made us realize that we had gone beyond mere survival. We were truly doing what we had dreamed about. Perhaps success might be within our grasp.

God has a way of using something as simple as a taxi to bring us back down to the realities of life. Yes, one had transported us to, and then another from, that elegant event. (By the time of the return trip, our aching feet had definitely taken priority over the hairdos as the rationale behind hailing a cab.) A couple of days later, the rain began. Desert Las Vegas takes on a completely different personality when the rain comes. Rain seems to arrive not as a sprinkle, but as a gully washer. We had gone to the Hilton Hotel for a breakfast meeting. The Convention Center was just one driveway width away. Normally, we would walk but a few steps from the side door of one into the side door of the other.

Not this day. By the time our meeting was completed, the rains had turned this driveway into a torrential river. The water was more than mid-calf deep. Now, these still were the days when we wore good, high-heeled shoes to COMDEX. After calculating the total worth of our two pairs of shoes, we decided that a taxi fare from the front of the Hilton to the front of the Convention Center would surely be far less. The best five-dollar (plus tip) decision of our careers.

The Epson party and subsequent meetings with a number of their executives meant that we returned to Little Rock with a heightened loyalty to that company. On the first day back we assembled and rallied our troops, attempting to imbue them with the same enthusiasm we felt for the future of Epson and the role we could play in it. We all knew that the major part of this relationship would entail our selling as many of the QX-10 units as possible. Volume was going to be the key, and we needed the help of an exuberant staff to accomplish this. Not only that, but as Ann indicated before, we needed to increase our visibility. "Location, location, location."

We did become visible. The site we selected turned out to be on one of the three busiest intersections in the city. It was a great place for retail exposure but not for automobile safety. The "wreck of the day" occurred so frequently on the street just beyond our parking lot that several of us enrolled in Red Cross Basic CPR! More than once accident victims were brought into our store, where we provided minimal first aid, limitless comfort, and a telephone for calls to relatives.

As initial occupants of this new store, Ann and I for the first time felt that this was really "our" place. The landlord finished it out just the way we wanted it, specifically for our needs. Once the move was completed, it was time for a Grand Opening Celebration, and celebrate we did! Penn and Bart had great fun helping us plan and prepare the offices to welcome the clients and prospects to our new home.

Fortunately we had included a large inventory room in our space design, since Epson soon announced two sales contests. The prize for the first was a February trip to Hawaii; then the leading QX-10 dealers in each region would be sent to *Japan* in April! This proved to be another turning point in our business. By this time both Ann and I had realized that the other was quite a determined woman, but these contests made us understand the extent of this quality we each possessed. We were going to do whatever it took to win both trips!

I will hasten to say that we stayed within our self-imposed boundaries of ethical and legal business practices and personal mores, but beyond that, it was full steam ahead. Our children and staff members were also swept into this wave of enthusiasm and became our most ardent cheerleaders. We ended up ordering so many QX-10s that they were stacked from floor to ceiling before they were sold, assembled, and delivered.

Retail was king, but we couldn't let go of our dedication to customer service and education. The happiest customers would be the ones who were best able to use their computers. (Then they, hopefully, would tell their friends about us, and their friends would buy from us, and we would be closer to our goal.) With that in mind we provided unlimited training to all, holding classes three evenings a week and even more if requested. Anyone who bought from us could attend as many of these classes as they desired and bring as many people as they wished. It takes little math to figure out how many hours per week this plan entailed, and it was not just the two of us but also our band of loyal co-workers who were involved. We were killing ourselves, but that was all right because specific objectives lay ahead, and we were determined to succeed.

"BULLETIN: Epson Mid-America's 'Hawaiian Escapade' February 19-25, 1984: winners announced." Yes, yes, we made it—we were going to Hawaii—a new adventure for us both!

Far below the windows on the right side of the plane, geography text outlines of a string of islands popped up from the monochromatic Pacific, each ringed by tan, white, azure, then navy blue. Sandy beaches, breaking waves, shallow water coral formations, and then the ocean depths once more. As the plane descended, we neared one island whose lush flora had evidently been invaded heavily by the needs and wants of mankind. Honolulu. Even its size could not eradicate the total beauty of this island. Diamond Head, Waikiki Beach—both just as I had pictured them. Then a sobering moment: there, down below, there was no doubt—Pearl Harbor. This is where it happened. We were afforded just a glance as the plane banked toward alignment for final approach, but I knew I would see it again.

Though now dwarfed by newer, towering high-rises, the tiny, pink, stately Royal Hawaiian Hotel sits undaunted where it has for years, at the edge of Waikiki Beach, like a majestic dowager queen. No longer the largest or the fanciest of the hotels, its elegance remains, however, unsurpassed and intact.

Ann and I were treated like royalty during our stay there. It would be easy to become accustomed to abundant fresh pineapples and other luscious fruit served on plates dotted with orchids. Although the food, the sun, the sand, and the water delighted my senses, the visit unexpectedly evoked emotions of a different type. Return to Pearl Harbor we did. Since the fifth grade I had had an intense desire to go there, to be there. I was not disappointed. Although the attack happened in 1941, before I was born, it became a part of the present as we stood on the dramatic memorial astride the USS *Arizona*. We watched as oil still seeped from below. To our right and to our left, the outline of the battleship, the tomb of so many.

Looking out over the peaceful harbor and encircling verdant hills, I tried to picture just what it was like on that December morning as the first wave of more than one hundred eighty fighters, torpedo bombers, dive bombers, and horizontal bombers zoomed toward their unsuspecting prey. My mind then flashed back to another scene. But a dozen years before, Mother and I had gazed out onto a green pastoral setting near Bastogne, Belgium, a site from the European Theater of the same war. The Battle of the Bulge had brought lumbering

Allied and German tanks and planes as vehicles of destruction—of property and of so many lives. The Hawaiian harbor and the Belgian hills had been beautiful before the attacks and were once again. In between, though, they were both sites of incomprehensible horror.

After the 1941 events of Pearl Harbor, so much more happened there, in the Pacific Theater of WWII. One day our entire group went to the American Cemetery in an extinct crater known as the Punch Bowl. There were row after row after row of fallen soldiers' graves. At the far end of the property are monuments, each bearing a map of a part of the Pacific action. There it was, a map of the Admiralty Islands, where my own father had been sent when I was but a month old. What a feeling to realize that our business and the work that we had put into it had unexpectedly given me the opportunity to connect with a distant part of my past.

The rest of our visit took us to a smaller island. The pre-trip literature described it beautifully: "Over eight million years ago, the volcano goddess Pele lifted an exquisite garden island from the sea...Kauai! Centuries of tides and trade winds followed to carve a flawless white-sand beach from the coastline...Poipu!" There we were, on the beach, in the ocean, and beside the pool, enjoying ourselves but always keeping close to the front of our minds the knowledge that an even larger goal was still ahead.

The trip to Hawaii was certainly superb, as we enjoyed each and every Mai Tai and pineapple chunk. However, the suspense was still building. We couldn't slack off now. Soon the results of the big contest were to be announced. We kept selling and selling and selling. Thank heavens this was a product we believed in and knew to be of excellent quality. Otherwise, we could not have in good conscience sold so many of them to the public—many to our friends.

"Congratulations on being selected for the 1984 'Epson' Dealers' Japan Holiday tour." Who was the most excited: Ann, Susan, Penn, Bart—or maybe the employees? All of us were maximally ecstatic! The children had been wonderful, right there beside us, even enduring the long hours and personal inconveniences as we marketed, sold, and delivered enough of the Epson QX-10s to reach our goals. Hopefully, they would remember life's lessons being played out in front of them:

- The bar had been set high.
- The reward was worth the effort.
- Family support in a major project is critical.
- A goal can be achieved only through the cooperation of all involved.

Yes, we had made it, and it felt so good!

Epson's Las Vegas party had been rather amazing. However, Ann and I were to find out soon that it was a pale preview of what was in store. It probably would have been wise for each of us to lose about twenty pounds before we left Little Rock, but we didn't know that at the time.

April 5, 1984. First stop, St. Louis, for The Grand Send-off, sponsored by our Epson regional distributor. We were pampered with a fancy hotel, a huge concierge-level room, and a lovely cocktail reception, all followed by a sumptuous dinner overlooking the nearby airport. We both remember vividly the artist who, during cocktail time, drew for each of us our first name in Japanese characters. (Later Ann and I had ours framed and placed on the walls of our offices, although we still aren't quite sure which says "Ann" and which says "Susan.") Yes, that was a wonderful evening, a tiny glimpse of what lay ahead.

The first full day was easy. Our only task was to board a 2:30 afternoon flight, which took us to Chicago in less than an hour. We could handle that. A brief orientation meeting and dinner—that was it. The next day was the big flight. It takes a long time to fly from Chicago to Tokyo, a very long time, even with a brief stop in Seattle. Our schedule indicated that we were to leave Chicago at 11:15 A.M. on Saturday, not arriving in Tokyo until 5:20 P.M. on *Sunday*. That made sense once we read that we would cross not only several time zones but also the International Date Line mid-Pacific and, thus, lose one day. Nevertheless, it was a long flight, and we tried not to think about the ones in First Class who were undoubtedly enjoying more luxurious arrangements than we had in Coach. I will admit, though, Japan Air Lines does attempt to make the experience as enjoyable as possible. The food, the beverages, the movie—all designed for our satisfaction. But it was a long flight.

We could not have predicted the abundance of experiences and feelings we would encounter during the following eight days. Our senses were sharpened by unfamiliar tastes, smells, sounds, sights, and, yes, even textures. Our minds were stimulated by fascinating, even futuristic, ideas. Our emotions were stirred by first-hand interaction with a culture whose history intersected ours in dark days for us both. Our egos were stroked. Our business acumen was enhanced by the observation of practices and processes. Our perspectives were broadened in many areas...but I really did miss my daughter, at just eight years old.

It is not an overstatement to say that our senses were bombarded during each waking minute. Cherry trees in full blossom exemplified the plethora of sensations that surrounded us. They were beautiful to behold in an explosion of white and pink, sweet to smell, and delicate to touch. Similarly, the abundant culinary selections presented to us were combinations of sensations. The smell, the taste, the arrangement, the texture, and even the sounds of dishes, some familiar, others not (but eaten on faith, usually) blended and resulted in a variety of gastronomic treats. Sights of the spreading megalopolis of Tokyo contrasted with those of the tiny rural villages; the elaborate temples with the tiny rustic roadside shrines; the famously prompt bullet train with the animal-drawn farm carts—all there for us to experience and to remember.

It was no secret that a certain number of hours had to be dedicated to product presentations. In one we were asked to do some really wild thinking and to write down our responses. "How light can a functional portable computer really be? Fifteen pounds? Ten? Seven? Five?" "How large a hard disk could this portable computer have? Five megabytes? Ten? Twenty?"

These numbers seemed like science fiction to us. "A computer as light as seven or five pounds? No way!" "A portable with a hard disk as big as twenty megabytes? Impossible!" Of course, it is now evident that they knew very well what the future of these products would be—because they had already designed and probably produced them.

During the ensuing years I have often thought about what

products really are on the drawing boards of companies such as Epson and how far outside the box they are thinking and designing. Ann and I put this experience to use within our business many, many times. We realized that, indeed, the Japanese are accustomed to looking at the "long term," not just the "short term." They are masters at planning far in advance and are interested in the effects that these plans might have far into the future.

One significant experience taught me a lot about myself as I put to test personal theories about trust in others and in my own abilities. One morning while we were in Tokyo I decided to explore the city on my own. Since Ann had other plans for the day, the arrangement worked well for us both. Lesson one: listen to sage advice. In this case it was "don't leave home [hotel] without it [them]." The "them" consisted of one's passport and a card with the name of the hotel written in English *and* in Japanese. I made sure that both, along with some money, were in my bag.

Having studied city guides and brochures, I decided that my destination would be a city botanical garden. Since we were in the spring of the year this seemed to be a logical choice, but in all honesty the target was less important than the process. I was challenging myself to strike out alone in a huge, strange city, whose language bore no resemblance to my own. I had read that the subways were safe and efficient (and clean!) and that the crime rate in Tokyo was very low. I hoped the guides were right.

How refreshing the early morning spring air as I walked to the subway station, which was conveniently near our hotel. First good sign: the station was immaculate. I took that as an affirmation that most likely the fact about a low crime rate would be true, also. I was counting on it. The Tokyo subways were not only clean but also extremely efficient and easy to use. Maps were posted prominently and were comprehensible even for me. The only help needed was fortunately minor and of a nature that transcended the massive language barrier. Pointing and nodding worked quite well and were useful not only in providing the information required but also in revealing to me the gentle politeness of these people. Lesson two: choose to have trust when it is merited. The reputations of the Japanese people and their subway system preceded my visit but certainly made my adventure a complete pleasure.

Lesson three: Japanese characters don't look a thing like the American alphabet. Emerging from the destination station, I peered at the street signs. They were there but did me not a bit of good. Not only could I not read them, I couldn't even write them down! OK—how to get from the station to the gardens and then *back to the station, the right station?* Resourcefulness and a sharpened sense of observation had to prevail. "One block, turn right at the yellow-colored building. Notice the work being done on the building where I turn left," etc., etc. It proved to be a challenge with rewards. The garden was lovely, and I returned to the proper station and to the hotel with no problem at all. Lesson four: trust yourself to strike out with confidence into unfamiliar territory, but do your homework first, and be observant.

It has become a lesson in self-discipline to limit the number of events and experiences from our trip to Japan. Perhaps some day we should write just about these. However, one in particular should not be omitted. I indicated earlier that the grandeur of the Epson party in Las Vegas was to be eclipsed by something that happened in Japan. In all honesty, there were several very nice events during the nine-day trip, but one almost defies description. Nevertheless, I shall try.

Mr. and Mrs. Ichiro Hattori, Chairman
and
Mr. and Mrs. Tsuneya Nakamura, President
of EPSON Corporation
request the pleasure of your company
for cocktails and dinner
on Saturday, 14 April, 1984, from 6:00 p.m.
at The New Otani, Tokyo, Japan.

This must have been the zenith, the epitome, the acme, the pinnacle of success—being invited to a reception by the Chairman and the President of Epson Corporation. Yes, we had worked hard, but this surpassed all expectation. The invitation was impressive, but the evening superlatively magnificent. This time it was even more difficult not to appear flummoxed, but we became actresses once more.

Sensing the importance of the evening, Ann and I again spent more time than usual in making sure that our attire and preparations were just right. No need for a taxi to protect our hairdos or soon-to-be-aching feet, since we were staying at The New Otani and only had to go down the elevator to the gala event. Soft background music from a grand piano greeted us as we joined the patient line of guests, queued to meet and shake hands with the hosts and their wives. Even I, caring little about celebrities (well…with the exception of Julie Andrews and John Elway, perhaps), was thrilled to realize that these were two of the most influential people in the computer industry in the entire world at that time…and they bowed to us! (Of course, each and every other person whom we had seen since we had gotten off the plane bowed to us, too. Great custom. We missed that once we returned to Little Rock!)

Cocktail time was brief but unhurried, providing an opportunity for all of us to find and take our assigned seats. Ann treasures the picture of her table, as she is seated beside this gorgeously handsome French Canadian fellow, who all week had been just as delightful as he was good-looking.

Printed menus at each place announced and detailed the *ten-*course meal that was to follow. No wonder there were *twelve* pieces of silver flatware and at least five stems of crystal set for each person. A small orchestra played as the "Foie Gras Nature en Abeille" was followed by the soup course, the fish course, and then the "Granite au Citron," a refreshing spot of sorbet to cleanse the palate before the presentation of the main course.

White-gloved, synchronized waiters had been tending to our needs throughout the evening, appearing and disappearing like efficient, well-trained ghosts. At this point each was standing at his assigned station awaiting a nod from the leader. As it came, a procession of trays streamed from the kitchen. They were cradled carefully until placed precisely, all at the same moment, onto awaiting racks. As had been true of almost every dish of the trip, the presentation was absolutely artistic; however, the mound in the center of each was somewhat nondescript in appearance. We referred to the *carte du jour*: "Filet de 'Matsuzaka' Boeuf en Croûte au Sel." In synchrony certain waiters struck the mounds. That seemed rather strange. Then they began cutting. The filets were served swiftly, on plates with "Légumes Assortis," Assorted Vegetables. That first bite remains emblazoned on my mind and in my taste buds. I never knew that beef could be that succulent or that melt-in-your-mouth tender or have the perfect flavor combination provided by the cooking method. It did. Sensing the ecstasy thus evoked, someone explained that this was Kobe beef—that the animals never walked outside their stalls—that their muscles were massaged by hand. The covering cracked by the waiters was a layer of salt applied before cooking. That combination is capable of effecting profuse salivation to this day.

Undoubtedly the next five courses were extraordinary, too, but I honestly don't remember them. Now, this lapse was not caused by too much wine. Yes, the wines were all wonderful, but the servers were careful to provide only one, maybe two, glasses of each type to each guest. Rather, the superior quality of the beef swept from memory all other details of the meal. Everything else—the laser light show, the dance band, the champagne—was anti-climactic after the Kobe.

That party was an amazing finale for a trip that taught us so much, from the time that the contest was announced until we returned to Little Rock. Three planes would bring us home. The first, a huge Japan Air Line jet, deposited us in Chicago. The second, a smaller Republic Air Line jet, took us from Chicago to Memphis. Finally, we were ready to board the much smaller Scheduled Skyways prop plane when the attendant announced that we were allowed only two carry-ons each. We each had three, including radios that we had bought for Penn and Bart in Tokyo. "Do you mean that we have come all the way from Tokyo with this and you say we can only take two on the plane?"

Resourcefulness came into play once more. "Ann, you stay right here at the gate." Since I was traveling in tennis shoes, I made excellent time sprinting to the Memphis airport gift shop. "Where are your tote or shopping bags? Oh, yes, here…I'll take two."

After running back to the gate, I completed the consolidation process before boarding began. "Here, put this and that into your bag. I'll put that and that into this one." Suddenly, our six packages had become four, the legal number for carry-ons. We felt that this process of going from the huge jet to a smaller jet to a small prop plane, with the accompanying problems, was God's way of trying to bring us down to earth even before we got home.

It had been a magnificent trip. However, nothing that we saw or experienced was as wonderful as the sight of my daughter's and mother's faces. We have a family tradition of "TYL" after a safe return. We pause and say, "Thank you, Lord."

Returning to the routine of our personal and business lives was easier than expected, since our families and co-workers were gracious enough to ask us to recount the events of our trip. At least, I think that they asked…at first, anyway. Whether or not they asked, they all heard enthusiastic descriptions of our visits and activities and even evidenced interest until we finally brought ourselves back to the responsibilities of the moment. Heightened enthusiasm for Epson and its current and future products insured that for the moment, we were on track to continue selling even though the contests were behind us. In all honesty, it was a test of will and cooperation for us not to let down, not to let ourselves lapse into a valley. We somehow pulled it off.

Ann and I found throughout our careers that employees had a way not only of keeping us in line, but also of eliminating any rudiment of inflated self-worth we might exhibit. In a year filled with such heady experiences, we undoubtedly needed deflating. Since 1984 was a decade year for me, the "big 4-0," they found a wonderful way of putting me in my place. How impressed I was when they, Ann, and the kids threw a birthday party for me, replete with gifts, balloons, and food! Upon unwrapping the gift from the staff, I was even more pleased since it evidently contained a plaque for my wall. "Wow, they must think I am pretty special," said my silent, inner voice.

"Go ahead—read it out loud!"

The Dolly Parton
Award
To

SUSAN DODSON
For Having 40
Of Something!!!

So much for my ego!

We continued with business as usual until several months later. I telephoned Ann from California saying honestly, "We are so happy to be *here*."

"I'm sure that you are, after that long drive across country. You are now with your family, and the Olympics are just beginning for all of you!"

"No, Ann, you don't understand. I am so happy to be here, to be alive! We had a terrible wreck today. We are all alive, and the injuries are relatively minimal. The van saved us, but it is in bad shape."

Just three days before, Penn, Mother, my niece Jennifer, and I had loaded our big, comfy van with luggage, food, games, and boundless excitement. We were going to the Olympic Games in Los Angeles, specifically because Jen's brother Andrew, a world-class oarsman, was to compete in rowing events. We were all rather thrilled, but Mother was ecstatic. Can you imagine the thrill of watching a grandchild compete in the Games?

Straight out Interstate 40 from Little Rock, all went well until soon after we crossed from Arizona into the Mohave Desert in California. A driver to our right lost control of her car and smashed into the van, throwing us down an embankment and into the fortunately wide median. I wrote a few days later, "[We] were thrown, jerked, pounded until finally, an eternity later, [the van] came to rest, crumpled, in a drainage ditch. By some miracle of God [its] wheels had barely missed an open culvert entrance and thus was able to avoid flipping."

At first glance, Mother and I seemed to be intact, then we heard a piercing child's cry from the back. Again I quote from my diary,

"Now fear of the unknown—broken bones? Lacerations? Twisted neck? Another miracle, none of the passengers was seriously injured." Penn did have to wear a neck brace and a bedroom shoe throughout the Olympics because of a twisted neck and a couple of cracked toes. Mother's ankle was sprained, but Jen and I just had a variety of bumps and bruises.

As the current adult-in-charge, it was natural for me to take control of responsibilities related to the accident. Mother, Penn, and Jennifer were loaded into an ambulance, which had come from the nearest town—forty-five minutes away. Relatively unscathed, I stayed on the scene and attended to the paperwork, van towing decisions, possession extraction, etc., etc. Finally, the kind trooper drove me to Barstow Hospital, where "my ladies" were sitting with ice packs and various limbs in states of elevation—and Penn with her neck brace. A rather motley-looking crew.

That night Penn and I shared a double bed. Before going to sleep she and I talked. "Remember how, before leaving Little Rock, we prayed for God to keep us safe on our trip?" There was a slight nod from the little head above the neck brace.

"Let's never forget that He did do just that—not quite in the way we had imagined or hoped for—but we all are safe, as are the people in the other car. Now let's thank Him once again for that."

Hopefully, in the darkened room she was unable to see that I blanched again at the thought of seeing our tire tracks so perilously close to that open culvert. How tempting to pull her closer and closer to me.

The next day we finally reached our destination, Beverly Hills, where the rest of our family awaited. I had been strong; I had been in control—until I saw my brother. Then I dissolved into tears in his strong, understanding arms. I wept for "what might have happened"— to his daughter, to mine, to our mother—but also for the relief that it didn't. I wept also for a crescendo of personal and professional responsibility that had been building inside without my realizing or admitting it. The wreck and my "big brother" allowed release.

Despite having lived through tragedies just four years earlier, Ann and I had both relapsed into the human tendency to take life and loved ones for granted. This accident made us evaluate once again how precious our friends and family—and yes, even business partners—really are. This book could not have been written had the van gone off the road about two yards sooner. The happy ending to this story is that nephew Andrew became a silver medalist, as his boat of eight was edged out barely, just barely, by the team from New Zealand.

I have one last comment on the trip to California. While there, I was able to visit the U.S. Home Offices for Epson and actually spoke with some people whom we had met while in Japan. The people there knew that we were Epson Dealers' Holiday winners, and that had a lot of clout back then. The red carpet was unrolled. The dream continued.

Custom Software Consultants, Inc., owners Susan and Ann displaying North Star products for the general accounting market.

New name — Computer System Integrators, Inc.; new logo, new location.

Ann and Susan boarding Japan Air Lines as winners in the Epson Dealers' Holiday.

Touring Epson facilities near Shiojiri, Japan.

With PCN friend Lorraine Ferraro at PCN Winners' Circle in Palm Springs, California.

New name—Medical Office Management Systems, Inc.; new logo; new location; new managers, Brenda Wright...

...and Joanne Kennedy.

Big plans for the MOMS Building.

"Dreamed about it—did it!"

Susan (center) with her mother, Dorothea Sudduth, and daughter, Penn Dodson.

Ann (standing) with Beverly, Brad, and Bart.

FLEXIBILITY

Ann speaks:

By the time Susan returned from the Olympics, our business was experiencing a slowdown. We were selling fewer computers and were going to have to be flexible again and try to figure out some new strategies.

Several competitors in our area began to sell the Epson computer, and new dealerships and franchises were just beginning to emerge. Sales of the North Star computer were diminishing as well, because the DOS operating system was becoming the standard not only for the personal computer but in businesses as well. The CP/M operating system was no longer widely accepted, as it had been in the past.

I was getting extremely frustrated because we were working harder and harder just to meet our overhead expenses. We were staying open on Saturdays and would even open the store if someone wanted to see a demo on Sunday. Many weeks we were working eighty hours, and sales had dropped off so dramatically that we were lucky to meet our dealership requirements. Larger dealerships were given merchandise costs far below our costs, and the only way we could keep our sales up was to cut our price to match that of the competition. When we did that, our margins often fell below eighteen percent. We were headed on a collision course.

For the first time in our business career, I was beginning to get scared. By that time we had a staff of *nine* to support, in addition to ourselves. I spent many sleepless nights wondering about whether we could meet payroll and our overhead expenses. We were working many hours and getting less for it, which added to the emotional drain and the fatigue we were experiencing. I thought many times about the Christian hymn that says, "He who begins a good work in you will be faithful to complete it." In my heart, I knew that God had placed us on this course and that he would not desert us. In my head, I wasn't quite so sure.

After a while, the emotion of fear usually does one of two things. It either immobilizes you, or it spurs you to action. In my case, I am too stubborn and impatient to let fear permanently put me out of action. For a while I can become immobilized, but then I get angry at myself. It is ok to have a "pity party," but for heaven's sake, put a time limit on it! I decided to fight back and persistently look for answers that I knew existed. The fact that we had not found them meant that we hadn't explored all avenues. Business can be compared to a giant chess game, and the moves are endless. The trick is to come up with the best move in one's mind before following through with the move. That strategy makes a bad move less likely.

The additional time we had to spend on our business in order to survive required less activity in the THEOS group. Not being able to find time to be as active in this worthwhile endeavor really tugged at our hearts; however, we were now deeply involved in building a business and keeping it. Also there were others to consider: our employees. They had placed their trust in us and placed their families in our care. Until one has walked in the shoes of a business owner, one is unable to grasp fully the awesome responsibility that goes along with it. Knowing that an employee is offering his or her talents and time to help build a dream and is also financially dependent on you is a sobering thought. Even though I was unable to give the time commitment to THEOS, good judgment told me that we had to continue to consider our employees first and foremost. We simply had to lessen our responsibilities and resign from being officers in THEOS. God was gracious to provide another person who was able to fill our shoes and become the next president of THEOS. Susan and I did all we could to help her quickly step into that role.

An event occurred one morning that helped to shape the destiny of our business. We spotted an advertisement in the newspaper that showed that Dillard's had started marketing the Epson computer. Their packaged price, complete with printer, was just slightly above our cost without the printer. We were devastated at the sight of this advertisement! Our initial reaction was just to "give up" and think about earning a living another way. I remember that Susan and I took our children Penn and Bart to dinner one evening and told them of our plans. We told them we thought they would be pleased to hear this news because our business often took us away from our motherly duties and they had to spend a lot of time at our businesses so that we could be with them.

I never will forget the horrified look the children had on their faces as almost in unison they stated, "Don't you dare give up. We don't mind the sacrifices because we are proud of you because you are both special. Not every mother could do the things that you have done, and we don't want you to stop what you are doing." That gave us the inspiration we needed. Somehow we would survive no matter what it took.

Even though Penn was only nine and Bart was fifteen, there was real wisdom in what they were saying. Every parent worries that they are not giving their kids enough of themselves, but it is reassuring when children confirm how proud they are of their parents. Despite the hard work, we always gave our children the very best we could. Being single parents gave us more incentive to do so. My son Bart spent endless hours at the office after school playing with computers. At least I knew where he was and didn't have to worry about his being a "latchkey" kid. This was a definite benefit in being a business owner. No one could tell the boss that his or her child could not be at the office. As an added benefit, today my son earns his living with computers. Had it not been for my business, he might have not been exposed to the latest technology and been as successful in his own career. We even took the kids to a COMDEX show one year, and they were always aware of how we earned our living. I feel this is very important in a child's education. Even though Bart had to spend the following three Saturdays doing yardwork at Catholic High

School as punishment for missing three days of school, he said it was still worth it. That was the punishment Father Tribou had administered when I had gone to him to seek his permission. He had never told me not to take Bart, but felt he had to take this stand.

Knowing what faith our children had in us, we began to do our research and investigate what segment of the computer marketplace had not been penetrated by everyone else. Although brief success had come with entering the retail marketplace, down deep we both knew that our skills lay elsewhere. Often things work out for the best. The retail business was never going to provide the long-term security that we were hoping to establish. Of course we had to complete this strategy as long as we could and as long as there was merchandise in our store. We had placed ads in the newspaper and had to fulfill obligations that were already in place. At the first opportunity, we would look for another niche that would provide a more secure and long-term future.

One day soon after this thought process, a man came into our store looking for a printer. We had exactly the make and model he was looking to purchase. It is funny how confirmation comes from the most unexpected sources. When I asked the man if he would like to purchase the printer, I will never forget his reply. He said that he could purchase the exact make and model in Memphis for twenty-five dollars less. The man will never know how much of a lesson he taught me that day. I replied as professionally as I could that maybe he ought to drive to Memphis if he could save that much money. He was only telling me this hoping that I would drop my price and discount my product. Discounting is very prevalent in the computer marketplace. I learned a very valuable lesson that day which I have continued to use all through my computer career. I tried never to discount a product; I would only provide "more for the money." Discounting can become a game that is endless. Value-added service is far more important and long lasting to a customer.

After doing some preliminary research on the computer application marketplace and doing some real soul-searching, we began to examine our strengths and weaknesses. This is a very necessary step for an owner of a business. The world is constantly changing, and a businesswoman has to learn to study trends and patterns that emerge as part of this change. If she does not, a business can become outdated and unable to meet current consumer needs and demands. The reengineering of a business is a very necessary process in insuring its long-term success.

While we were in this decision-making process, we learned another valuable lesson. During another Epson dealer trip to Hawaii, we went on a whale-watching adventure with the group. Whales are very active and fortunate observers can see a spectacular show when the whales roll to the surface of the water, slapping it with their flukes. Since on this particular day the water was a bit rough, I decided to take a pill to prevent motion sickness. We were expected to be out on the water for about two hours. Thirty minutes into the trip I became deathly ill and was unable to hide my seasickness. Not knowing whether it was better to be in the ship's head or hanging over its rail, I made a steady path from one to the other. There was no choice but to endure since the boat had to stay out a set amount of time. My savior was a very kind man who had me sit beside him and who literally talked me through the next hour and a half. I have never been sicker in my life. At that moment, death would have provided a welcome relief. As soon as my feet stepped onto steady shore, I was instantly okay.

From that day to this, I have used this experience as a measuring tool when I have faced a difficult situation. Nothing could be as bad as that day on the boat. Those who know me know exactly what I mean when I refer to my "whale" story. We have used that incident to make sure we maintain perspective.

Susan and I realized that every product we sold had an educational component, and we seemed to do better with professional people. We were not as equipped to deal with the average consumer and could not anticipate their needs as well. Our success had largely come from specific industries and individuals who were using computers to augment their professional careers and lifestyles. Our philosophy had always been to be flexible and have at least two products to sell, but maybe now it was necessary to change from that former thinking. One day as we were discussing our options, I asked Susan

what industry we were most familiar with. She answered as I expected when she said, "the medical profession." Not only had she been
married to a doctor, but her brother was also one. She used to make
house calls with her grandfather when he practiced medicine in a
small town in Kentucky. I had been working for a large pediatric clinic
at the time of my husband's death, and we had sold a medical package in earlier years. The medical profession was our common thread.
I remember saying, "Let's get away from our former thinking and try
to do one thing and do it better than anyone else." That one thing
should be marketing to the medical marketplace!

The only computerization that was widespread in the medical
community at the time were those clinics that had purchased large
mainframe computers. Due to their expense, only the largest of clinics were able to afford them. Since Arkansas is a rural state and comprised of many small practices, we realized that there could be a
definite niche in this marketplace. Microcomputers were now becoming affordable for physicians and were less expensive on a monthly
amortized basis than the costs of service bureaus. Besides, doctors
who used service bureaus were reliant on information which was
usually not real time-dependent information. Only an in-house system
can provide instant access to information while patients are still in
the clinic. Now that computer systems were becoming affordable to
doctors, we felt this was exactly the marketplace we needed to pursue. A term that was beginning to be used during those days was a
"vertical" marketplace. No longer were we going to try to meet the
needs of many, but rather concentrate on the needs of a highly specialized marketplace which was to be found within the healthcare
industry.

Now that we had made our decision, it was time to do our final
research to find a really great medical package that would meet the
needs of the average physician. First we had to choose the package,
and then we had to decide what operating system and hardware to
use. We also knew that it should be multi-user, because a physician
could not benefit from having a PC on just his desk. It was more efficient for several people in a physician's office to be able to operate from separate terminals to perform various functions of the office.

This type of computer system would have to be more sophisticated than we had been dealing with in our other experiences as business owners.

Susan began exhaustive research into finding an excellent medical package. Her background in helping computerize an orthopedic clinic as an office manager certainly did help in this search. Finally, she had narrowed the field to two or three options. All involved packages that ran on the UNIX operating system. We now knew how to spell this word, which we heard for the first time at that computer convention we attended in 1981. Our notes stated that the leaders had said UNIX was the operating system of choice in a multi-user environment. The conference also unveiled the IBM PC which was used as a single-user computer. Even then, the experts had realized that there would be a place for both types of computers and operating systems.

Now that we had a little more direction on the type of software we wanted to market, it was time to find the hardware that supported the operating system. Our research told us that Bell Labs had created the UNIX operating system in 1969, and that the only computer hardware able to support this operating system ran under the AT&T hardware. Coincidentally, AT&T had just announced a new product called the 3B2 computer, which was going to be presented at a large computer show which would be held in Las Vegas at the COMDEX show. We would attend the show and also check out medical software packages displayed there. We were now renewed with excitement. Our passion had been refueled, and we had our spark back to make new discoveries that would put us on a path to success.

As an act to hedge our bet somewhat, we decided to get in touch with AT&T before the actual show. We had learned that making preliminary contacts can make all the difference. Just as we had hoped, a young man was eager to meet us and show us the product line. We even got invited to a special showing, which would provide added contacts that we would need to secure a source for hardware and go through the necessary steps of becoming a reseller.

When we finally arrived in November 1984, we were well prepared to visit specific booths and to make intelligent choices for our

newly directed business. Since one hundred thousand people attended that year, it was much more difficult to see all the prominent
booths we had set out to see. Computers were really coming into
their own now, and several early laptops were also featured. We remained focused, though, and made sure we visited the medical software booths and saw the different packages exhibited. Our
assignment was to pick one package and make sure we had fully explored all its features and benefits. After visiting several booths and
seeing several demos, we decided to represent a software practice
management system called the Wallaby system. It seemed to be the
most flexible and contained most of the ingredients a busy medical
office would need. We were fascinated by the name and discovered
that one of the owner's children had liked the name. Based on that,
Wallaby was born. We were especially pleased to see its reporting
capabilities and made arrangements to become a reseller for this product. It also was able to handle the many new requirements given by
insurance companies for payment. Back then, we had no idea how
important that would become. This was before managed care requirements were initiated.

     We also visited our contact at AT&T and made arrangements to
become a reseller for their hardware. Having attended the premier
showing of the product which was held in another location, we were
well equipped with the information we needed to proceed. Then we
were able to spend time just enjoying the rest of the show and visiting as many booths as our feet would allow us to visit. In those days,
walking shoes were not in vogue, and I now have the feet to prove
that I was vain enough to go along with this trend. It was years later
that sneakers became an acceptable and necessary item for attending shows.

     For the sake of nostalgia, we attended the Epson booth to see
some of the people we had worked with and to renew old acquaintances. We were surprised to see all new faces and found that we had
already lost some of our original contacts. Because Epson was a Japanese company, this is not surprising. Technology had begun to change
for Epson, and they were looking at new intros into the market and
had just come out with a version of their new laptop computer. We

did make a valuable contact there with a lady who was looking for people to write industry-specific books for Epson. When I found out the writer would be compensated, I volunteered Susan's time to write *Medical Office Applications Using Your Epson.* I knew she possessed the wherewithal for it. She later spent all of her Thanksgiving time writing and was unable even to go to her home in Nashville because of the deadline imposed by the publisher. I really felt bad for taking her away from her family that year and committing her to such a labor-intensive project. We were definitely grateful for the money she later received for the project, as it came at a very good time in our business.

When we left the COMDEX meeting that year, we felt we were on our way to re-inventing our business and starting a whole new strategy which was poised for success. We had decided it would happen, we were willing to work hard to make it happen, and we could visualize our success as it happened. These are necessary ingredients in making any venture successful. All we had to do was to refine our marketing strategy and start getting prospects to sell. With God's help we could do it. He had proven that many times in the past and would again in the future. We had no idea at that time what might be in store for us, but we had another entrepreneurial dream in our hearts.

Now that we had changed our focus, it was time once again to add another name to our business. I have always been a believer that a name should state what a person does. We settled on the name Medical Office Management Systems, Inc. Our name indicated our mission statement. We computerized medical clinics. Later, we changed our name one more time, this time to MOMS, Inc. It was catchy and it gave a warm feeling to others. After all, everyone trusts a mom, don't they? A mom gives support and understanding in all that she does. The name was now perfect! We had it right, and it was what we were going to stick with. The only thing left to do was to change our location to a business setting. We were no longer interested in people just appearing at our place of business without an appointment. This change would certainly not have to delay our marketing. We had already learned the key was flexibility. It was now the end of the year, and soon we would begin a new year with a new product.

In January we began to market our product to clinics in the Little Rock and surrounding areas. After several demos, we managed to develop some very qualified prospects. We also attended a medical seminar and came up with more leads. It seems we were right; medical offices were getting very interested in computerizing their own offices and being able to have information at their fingertips. One thing I was not prepared for was the fact that this marketplace had a long sales life cycle. It was not unusual for a prospect to take six to twelve months to make a decision. At least we were on the beginning curve of a new business opportunity.

At long last, we had an interested prospect that appeared to be ready to make a decision. The prospect was a two-doctor OB/GYN clinic. The office manager was also the wife of one of the doctors. She was extremely astute and really did her homework in picking a computer system. I will always remember when she asked the question, "Can I call some of your references to check out the system?" Without even flinching, we told her that this was a new product for us in this area, but that we would be happy to get her a reference in another state. We were holding our breath that the software company really did have an OB/GYN clinic as a reference, as they had not been in business very long. They just had to rescue us. What would we do if they were not able to help us? We refused to think in negative terms at this point. We had come too far for that. Fortunately, the office manager of that clinic gave a very good referral, and our prospect seemed satisfied after having talking with her. I later learned that the clinic out of state was a "beta" site and the system had not been installed for very long. That didn't matter though; our prospect had decided to give us a chance. She will never know how much that shaped the very destiny of our business. She had faith in us, and that carried us through many rough spots in the infancy of our newly founded vertical marketplace.

Once the sale was made, not only did the customer need training, but we were going to have to go to New Jersey to receive our initial dealer training as well. Since Susan was the more technical partner, and I had sole responsibility for ordering all products and conducting business operations, it was an easy decision for her to go.

The OB/GYN office manager also wanted to attend the training class. This was probably a very smart decision on her part since her clinic was our first installation. She would have the benefit of being trained by the experts and the authors of the software. It was my job to stay at home and run the business and develop new leads for Susan's return.

I really didn't believe the sale was real until I delivered the contract and received the down payment. Only then could I believe that our reasoning for approaching this new marketplace really was on target. The closing of the deal has always been my favorite part of the business. Now I had to figure out how to duplicate this process many times over to keep sales coming in and build security within the company. It was a challenge I was ready for, and I welcomed it with open arms.

EVOLUTION

Susan speaks:

The hotel fire alarm blared sometime in the sleep-infused early hours. Curiosity led me to get out of bed and look through the peephole. Smoke! Real firemen in full gear—just outside my door!

Knock-knock. "Are you OK? We will need to evacuate!"

I grabbed a jacket and ran across the hall to the room of my friend, who was also the office manager of our very first Wallaby client—and the wife of one of the doctors. *Bam-bam!* "Judy, are you all right? We need to get out." About then one of the firemen appeared at the door.

Looking at Judy he politely said, "Ma'am, you're going to have to put on more than that! It's cold out there!"

Her pink pajama set was lovely but would certainly not offer sufficient protection against the cold of a New Jersey February night—or early morning. Bundled, we obediently headed to the stairwell where we stayed until allowed to go into the lobby. Then we were told that the fire had been isolated to one rooftop-heating unit and that there was more smoke than fire.

Ann speaks:

This is an actual account of the experience Susan and the office manager had when they attended the training in New Jersey in February of 1985. The cold temperatures really added to the trauma of this experience. Susan and I both realized that the trip to New

Jersey was going to be an exciting event, but we didn't realize that a "trial by fire" would be part of that experience.

Because the incident occurred during the night, neither Susan nor the office manager had much sleep. Despite that fact, the class was very informative. It proved to be exactly what the manager was hoping to find in a medical package for her husband's practice. It gave Susan even more confirmation that she had made the right decision in picking this particular medical package. When she returned, Susan had acquired the knowledge and expertise to train the next customer, and we were well on our way to having a satisfied customer. Or so we thought at the time. Little did we know how much technical assistance would be involved before we could use her as a reference.

First we had to do the installation and get the clinic personnel trained and comfortable with the system. As it happened, there was a very technical and talented individual who had come to us because his business had taken a bad turn and he was seeking employment. He was brilliant as a programmer and had developed good usage of the UNIX operating system. For whatever reason, he had come to us at a time when we were in dire need of his technical expertise. Our first installation was going to require his knowledge and familiarity with the operating system. We had never done an installation in a multi-user environment with several terminals and printers. We hoped we had not bitten off more than we could chew, but we had already collected enough of the money that there was no turning back now. Being in the computer industry required being a pioneer, and we were certainly in that category at this point. After several days and several mishaps, we had finally installed the computer system and everything was properly handshaking. (*Handshaking* is a term used to explain that all peripherals and devices were working with one another and with the main server.)

One thing for which we were unprepared was the number of support calls that needed to be handled with a medical environment once the computer system was installed. Birthing a computer system is not unlike birthing a child. We had birthed this child, and there were the usual number of new parent responsibilities and worries that went with it. We also realized that we were going to need an application support person to be standing by when customers had questions—and there were going to be plenty of questions. I used to think it was because microcomputers were in their infancy that so much technical support was required, but I have changed my mind and now believe that it is because technology is always superior to the intelligence of human beings. It is called the ESTO factor, "Equipment Superior to Operators." We had to add another element to our business, *patience*. During all the years we were in business, the need for patience was always present.

We began some seminars in which we touted that we had the computer prescription for medical office efficiency. We pointed out the many benefits of having an in-house computer system that was tailored to meet the needs of a particular clinic rather than expecting the clinic to conform to its structure. Another benefit we stressed was instant access to information as it was needed by the clinic and the patient. A clinic could even print a walk-away bill so the patient knew exactly what was owed, and in most cases this would get the patient to make a payment at the window before leaving. Cash flow increased and people paid bills more readily when they received computerized statements rather than old-fashioned statements. The computer system could send out hundreds of statements in a brief period as compared to other methods which were far more laborious. We always found seminars to be excellent sources for getting prospects with a ratio that was far higher than any other method of selling.

A business owner has to wear many hats. I have often told people that in the early years of our business we had to run everything, "including the vacuum cleaner." When we were doing demos, Susan wore a beeper so she was always in touch with the office. It was really difficult to be in two places at once until we had a competent person who was fully trained to help with software support calls. We were also wearing the hats of salespeople, support people, and operations managers. We always prayed that we would not get beeped during a demo because it could prove embarrassing. We wondered what went on in the minds of prospects when that happened.

By May of 1985, we had managed to sell three more clinics and get them installed and trained. We were really getting busy, and it was fun knowing that we were at the beginning of a new trend. At one of our busiest times, we received a call from a corporate office of AT&T in New Jersey. They had heard about our success installing the Wallaby software system on the AT&T computer and wanted to visit us. We were naturally thrilled at the prospect of our notoriety and agreed to allow them to come down.

We agreed to meet the two ladies at the hotel where they were staying, and they had invited us to dinner. We were completely unprepared for the conversation and the message they had come to deliver. The older lady told us that they were very impressed with our reputation, and they wanted to visit the first clinic that we had installed. She also stated that AT&T was looking to co-label the medical software and sell it as a complete system throughout the country. I will never forget the next comment she made. She told us "to step aside and let the big boys take it from here." We were a small company and were no match for a large corporation. After recovering from her statement, we politely replied that we were going to continue doing what we were doing but that we appreciated the warning.

We later decided that this was a sign to us that we must be doing something right. It's been said that a true sign of being a pioneer is to realize that there are arrows being shot at your back. Sometimes they stick and they hurt, but the test is in continuing to persevere. The anger we felt after the statement made to us by the "big boys" and delivered by the "ladies" spurred our efforts more than ever before. We had decided that these corporate people were not going to prevent us from doing what we loved. After all, this is America, and we are allowed to become all that we can be. Small business is supposed to be the heart of America!

We received a call from the local university medical center asking that we begin a program to train residents on our software. Doctors have intense training in medical school in order to prepare to become physicians, but very little training in business applications. We felt it was a great opportunity for us to become known and have the residents see our system so they would remember us upon graduation. That is exactly what did end up happening, because we had many of them as customers over the years. We also displayed at their residency convention and got to know many of them on a first name basis. The medical profession is very loyal, and word of mouth is very important in networking. We learned that lesson early on in our business careers.

The next few months there was a flurry of demos, installations, more demos, and more installations. We even managed to display in a Business Technology show in July at a downtown convention location. By August, we had sold so many systems that we won a reseller trip offered by Wallaby to Atlantic City for outstanding sales performance. Even though we were thrilled to be winners, we were almost too busy to take the trip. It was as if we were in another time zone, trying to beat out the enemy. In this case our enemy was AT&T. Will Rogers made a very powerful statement when he said, "Even If You're On The Right Track, You'll Get Run Over If You Just Sit There." There are times when this statement is especially applicable, and it is a motto that we adopted early on in our business and one we continued to exercise throughout our business careers.

The local newspapers contacted us, and we were fortunate enough to be featured in the business sections of both state papers. It was fun to be accepted as a successful business owner, and the fact that we were women made it even more exciting. There were not a lot of women-owned businesses during the eighties, and we were pleased to be among them. We liked the feeling of becoming role models and mentors to other women who might follow in our paths. Early on, before we had started a business, other women gave us encouragement and inspiration to start our business. My mother had been my mentor, and she had given me a precious gift in the process. I am a great believer in giving back to society when the opportunity arises. This way the cycle is completed, and the circle remains unbroken. We became known as the "computer ladies" and were happy to serve in this role.

Of course some distributors couldn't get used to the fact that we were the owners and not the employees. A certain distributor, who is no longer in business, just wouldn't accept the idea of our being a woman-owned business. He used to call and ask to speak to Mr.

Baskette. When I told him that I was Ms. Baskette and was one of the owners, he refused to give up. He finally said in desperation, "May I please speak to the man in charge?" Needless to say, I quit doing business with his company and was totally turned off by his attitude. I had never allowed being a woman to stand in my way of treating both sexes on an equal basis. I was never caught up in women's liberation movements. I felt there was an equal opportunity for both sexes working side-by-side, complementing each other's abilities. I will admit that being a business owner made it easier to exercise this philosophy.

Even though you are on the right track, you can still get sidetracked. This was exactly what we allowed to happen when we hired another salesperson. Because she had some background in construction and manufacturing, we thought it might be fun to explore another vertical marketplace. We again did our research and came up with a great construction package. It seemed to be a logical conclusion to do so. We managed to install two packages in two different companies and do all of the necessary training and work involved in getting them up and going on a computerized system. One of the companies continued to have problems, and there seemed to be nothing we could do to get it right. We ended up giving one of the companies their money back for the price of the software. I will always believe it was because our expertise as a company was not geared for this industry, which is what it takes to be successful. If you can't think like an industry, you cannot serve them in their best interests. Because our expertise was in the medical environment, we knew the problems and challenges of that industry; therefore, we were able to help them resolve their special challenges and needs. After the construction instances, we never deviated from our focus. We had learned an expensive lesson, and we became much more astute because of it.

In the fall, I lost a very dear friend. Our husbands had been friends and we had all attended the same church. When I attended her funeral, I was not prepared for the experience I had. As I sat in the same church pew where I sat five years before for my husband's funeral, I reflected on all that had happened during the years since his death. God had provided so much for my family and me. He had given us a path to follow and the resources to do it. Because we had relied on Him and utilized the resources from deep within, Susan and I had been able to build hope for the future. This process is not automatic. We had to constantly ask for His guidance to help keep us on the right path and encourage us when we became discouraged. The most valuable part of prayer is realizing that God is listening, but He is waiting for our mouths to utter our requests. He wants to give us our hearts' desires, but He also wants us to give him the credit for the gift. Even though the answers may not come exactly according to our requests, no sincere prayer is ever unanswered.

Attending Loretta's funeral gave me a confirmation of this lesson. I was not prepared to feel as emotional as I did. I even had difficulty at one point catching my breath, and I could feel my heart racing beyond its normal beat. I realized that we never get over losing someone we love, we merely adjust to their absence. Loretta had lived a good life, and I was reminded of the fragility of life and how close we are at all times to death. It is up to us to live a life that is pleasing to God so that we are ready when our call comes. I realized at that moment that I had not completely healed from Bill's death, and that there was further rehabilitation ahead. It would take several more years before I would become completely healed, if ever.

It was time to attend another COMDEX. Where had the year gone? Of course we knew the answer, but it was November again and the year would be gone very soon. It would be interesting to see what computer advances we would see at this COMDEX. We knew that AT&T would be displaying, and we were curious to know if they would also be showing our medical package that they had co-labeled. For this reason, we felt it was a convention we could not afford to miss.

Once we arrived at the convention, we were blown away by the number of exhibitors and attendees. The computer convention was no longer restricted to the Convention Center, but two additional hotels were now being used for display of vendors. The attendance that year was approaching one hundred twenty thousand people. Another reason for attending the show was that we were able to meet with other resellers who were our peers in other parts of the country and compare stories of our businesses and learn from one another. We were able to form an alliance and stay in touch with these same people as time progressed. Since we were located in different parts of the country, our colleagues weren't really competitors, so this took the feeling of competition out of the equation. They became our business friends and we formed deep relationships. We were all in the same business and could openly discuss our successes and our failures.

As we expected, AT&T was displaying the medical package in their booth and would be marketing the product by the following spring. We knew we had to work harder than we had ever done before, even though their marketplace would be in much larger geographical locations. We felt we had a little time before their presence became known in Arkansas, and we decided to use that time to get more and more installations in our own home state. We had been down the road of being "squeezed" by competition before and didn't want to let it happen again. It was not fun experiencing defeat after experiencing success in a growing business. As business owners, we realized that we must always appreciate our success and never take it for granted. Success can be a fleeting thing and can be taken away so easily; one can never become complacent or take one's mind off the bottom line.

Wallaby also had a wonderful booth at this COMDEX show. It was nice seeing the Wallaby team, who had become our business friends by that time. I always like to get to know the people I work with on a face-to-face basis. When dealing with a national company, it is great to have that relationship. It helps in day-to-day situations and when facing problems together. I also believe it is important to have fun while working. It helps prevent burnout and monotony, and makes each new adventure more precious. Wallaby must have felt the same way because that year they decided to treat their top dealers and take them to dinner in a limo. We were one of those dealers, and it really added a lot of memories to the trip. We were treated like royalty that night as a reward for our successes.

When we returned, we had a renewed sense of energy and were

able to tackle any situation that arose. We were determined to end the year with a bang, and we certainly did that. Our system installations were now growing in number, and it was getting to be fun doing it. When a business is on a success track, it seems to continue rolling and building on other successes. That was the formula we were using, and it was coming day by day and week by week. We had become entrepreneurs and were enjoying every moment of the experience. The year 1985 had been a wonderful year for us. Even if the next year was not successful, no one could take away the success of that year.

TRAINS TO PLANES

12

Susan speaks:

In keeping with Ann's railroad analogy, it did seem that we entered 1986 barreling along at Bullet Train speed. COMDEX 1985 had inspired and enabled us to focus even more directly on the core competency of our business. We were to serve the medical industry and only the medical industry. No more agriculture, no more paint contractors, no more insurance companies, no more motorcycle shops. (We probably have not even mentioned that one, but it is just as well.)

With the renewal of this perspective, our business continued to expand so that our theme for 1986 could have been a line from Libba Cotton's song: "freight train going so fast." Reviewing our calendars for that year has, frankly, left me exhausted. Prior to that year, it had been easier to balance work, family, friends, church, social engagements, and cultural events. Each of these was important and could be thought of as an individual car on the train. Then work required more time. Since the children were older, their activities were more numerous. Church, friends, and social and cultural activities should not be cut out. Ann and I found that we not only were on that train but also were having to become more creative than ever to keep it from jumping track. A derailment could be disastrous in all parts of our lives.

The exponential increase in business could be attributed not only to our focus on the medical profession but also to an added sophistication in our marketing plan. Ann and I built on past experience. It has been shown that we had realized the importance of carrying through one project or line of business, not dropping it until another was firmly in place. We knew to hold on to that which was proving successful while simultaneously looking for the next field of focus. Up to this time, the clinics had been sold one by one. That had been fine; however, it was evident that selling to a larger entity would enable us to take leaps instead of baby steps. Fortunately, though, we were either wise or lucky enough this time not to let go of the current plan. We developed parallel and complementary marketing strategies.

"AHEC demo—8105b—Ed. II Bldg." Even looking back after fifteen years, I know that the entry on January ninth was reminding me to appear at the University of Arkansas for Medical Sciences, Education Building II, Room 8105b, to present a demo to the administrators of the Area Health Education Centers. It was one of the most grueling and challenging demo experiences of my career, and well it should have been. Those in charge were in search of what they considered the best computer system to manage data in all AHEC offices scattered throughout the state. UAMS had already developed a well-deserved reputation for this AHEC program, designed to provide training for family practice residents. Besides, this state-controlled university is not unlike its counterparts. Budgets are tight, and value for dollars spent is paramount. Function, money, reputation, value—all had to be considered carefully. No wonder I was grilled that day.

Of course, that first demo was but the beginning of a long process. Since this is a state agency, the proposal had to be entered as an official bid. This step added to the torment. "What if we are the best system, but number two is just a few dollars less?" *Thrilled* was the emotion shared not only by Ann and me but also by the staff members when the official notification arrived. We were the winners—our first multi-site contract!

Once again, we felt like the barking dog who chased the car—only we caught it. As mentioned before, these sites were all over the state, from Jonesboro in the northeast, to Fayetteville in the northwest, to El Dorado in the south, to Ft. Smith in the far west, to centrally located Pine Bluff. Great, we have the contract, but now we have to install and train and support all of these sites! Again, flexibility became key, and perhaps even the byword of our staff and families. It had never been more important for us all to pull together, and we did just that. This is truly the type of landmark in the life of a company that can be a make-or-break situation and should not be taken lightly. Once the contract had been awarded, if we had not had the full cooperation of our staff, Ann and I could have been ruined. We could not have fulfilled it by ourselves. We did not have to, since the team made it happen.

Fulfillment of this contract would illustrate a physical law that I studied while a biology major at Sweet Briar College. It applies to both the biological and business worlds. The more complex an entity, the more different types of specialized units are required for optimum functionality. Hydras and jellyfish have no need of brain, liver, lung, or muscle cells. We humans depend not only on the existence of all of these cells but also their harmonious interaction and cooperation. Ann mentioned the fact that when we first formed our company, we ran everything "including the vacuum cleaner." Gradually we added employees. By the time of the AHEC sale, it became evident that not only did all the employees have to work together, but also that success was now dependent upon people with specialized knowledge. Our technician was excellent, but we would have starved if he had been in charge of marketing.

Following close on the heels of the AHEC contract came another, similar in that it involved a number of sites but quite different in other aspects. Uro-Tech was a company formed by the collaboration of a number of people and business concerns. In contrast to AHEC, which focused on the generalized field of family medicine, Uro-Tech concentrated on the highly specialized field of lithotripsy, a non-surgical procedure for the elimination of kidney stones. Support of AHEC sites required travel, but all within the state of Arkansas. By contrast, although one lithotripsy site was in Little Rock, the corporate office where most of the training took place was in Houston. Another site was in Dallas. There were other locations as well. For the first time we were more than just an Arkansas company. We had expanded our horizons by crossing the state line. Before this contract, we were able to drive to all our sites. With Uro-Tech began our increasing dependence upon the airlines, with all of the accompanying joys and challenges. During the term of this contract, it was not at all unusual for me to take a 7:00 A.M. flight to Dallas, train all day and return home at 9:00 P.M..

This evolution strengthened another side of the business, one that interfaced with our personal lives. Although Ann and I had always cooperated with each other, as the company took this leap in scope we came to depend upon each other as never before to help out with each other's families. Penn was secure in the fact that, even when I had to be away on an all-day or even an overnight trip, Ann would be there to retrieve her, feed her, and provide a place to sleep. Similarly, when Ann had to be away I was a temporary surrogate mother for Bart. Then we all knew that if we both had to be away at the same time, all we had to do was to call my mother, and she would be here. At first we had to do this only at COMDEX time, but by 1986 these requests were becoming more and more frequent. (It was evident that this was certainly no burden for her.)

After we had taken the initial foray onto foreign soil, it seemed that our company's reputation expanded, providing us with an increasing number of out-of-state opportunities, not all of them sales. An invitation from AT&T to speak on computer systems in medical practices found me flying to my first (and so far only) visit to Amarillo, Texas. The people were delightful, but the water was some of the most distasteful ever. I found that not even a shot of good scotch could make that water palatable. Nevertheless, I presented "The PERKS of a Computer in a Medical Practice." In retrospect this many years later, I realize that the basic premises delineated at that time are patently relevant to practices today. I began by projecting a picture of a nun onto the screen. Its caption read, "If God had meant for us to have computers, he never would have given us brains. That's what I say." My premise was that God has given us both brains and computers and that we are now to use both. At one point I quoted a Dr. Cecil Hart, "If you don't already have an efficiently run office...you're not going to achieve perfection because you installed a computer." With each system installed, we found out the profound truth of that statement. Some brought us joy and others brought unbelievable headaches.

Years before, in 1977, one event left an indelible imprint on my life. My husband and I took our first trip to Colorado. Ever since, part of my heart beats there…and the rest of my body follows as often as possible. How thrilled I was when in 1986 AT&T invited me to conduct training courses for them in Denver! Remember, they had told us earlier that we might as well get out of the way since they were going to run over us in this medical computer field. Evidently, their tune was changing since they were coming to *us* to *train* their people. It might seem that I was going out to empower the enemy. Not so. We knew that we would still do better than they could in this field. They were hoping to turn telephone salespeople into seasoned medical computer salespeople with only a week of training sessions.

Lack of maturity on the parts of many of the trainees was evident. Their hangovers on Day Two were my first clue, but that was followed closely by their blatant attempts to throw me off track. Hey, I "knew my stuff" and was determined to hold the class together. Besides, I could calmly look out onto the Rockies, my source of inspiration. Also, I wanted to do well so that AT&T would invite me back. I won; they requested my return. In all honesty, some of the groups were attentive, but none was a threat to MOMS!

Even though 1986 saw us expanding to multi-site projects, fortunately Ann and I realized that the single-site sales were continuing to be our bread-and-butter. We stayed in touch with existing clients while courting prospects. This basic business wisdom served us well. That "warm and fuzzy" feeling fostered by the name MOMS helped build a network of loyal and wonderful clients. To facilitate this process we designed and published the first issue of our newsletter, *MOMS at Work*. Well, "published" might be stretching it a bit; perhaps "printed" is a more accurate word. The newsletter consisted of text and very basic graphics produced by a dot matrix printer printed on a single page and then photocopied and mailed. We were grateful for the assistance of "Technical Director: Bart Baskette" (who was sixteen at the time). This medium was effective in allowing us to reach out to our "family," not only to communicate with them but also to provide helpful technical and application information and advice. We tried to infuse a bit of fun also. "It was all play and no work at the Capital Club the evening of May 21st because this was a night of fun!! As you know, on that day Computer Systems Integrators (parent company of Medical Office Management Systems) celebrated its FIFTH anniversary...As our second five years begins, we have renewed our commitment to providing each of you the very best of professional services within our area of expertise, just as you do the same for your patients."

Face-to-face communication was important as well. We enjoyed being with our clients but also knew the value in helping them meet each other and share experiences. In establishing an End-Users' Group and hosting regular meetings, we evidently had confidence that our clients were satisfied in most instances. Otherwise, meetings such as these would lapse into nothing but "gripe" sessions. "You think that was bad...let me tell you what happened to me!!!" When a hint of negativity did creep in, we always did our best to defuse it, then turn it into a positive. "Yes, you did have that problem. Now let's go through the steps that were taken to solve it!"

The burgeoning strength of MOMS can be attributed in large part to Ann's marketing savvy, but she was (and still is) just one person. Even she could not have taken our sales to the 1986 volume if she had not also had the enthusiasm and desire to mentor our fledgling sales force. Each month she and her crew would "shake the trees and rake the leaves"—and some months it took a lot of shaking before we could start on the raking. Still they persevered...and kept the training team "on the road again" and again and again. That was OK—we were growing.

Even though we did have others on staff, very often the sales cycle would begin with me and end with Ann. Being more familiar with the software and the functioning of medical offices, I was the one to do the initial demo and needs analysis. Once the words "how much?" were uttered, I began to sweat. Luckily it soon became very easy to say, "It will be better if I take this information back to the office and then provide you with an accurate proposal, with a design for your system and the cost involved."

That sounded so much better than the truth: "I have no idea how much—Ann will have to tell you."

For the most part, this process worked well. I would load up a computer, go to the clinic, demo, and return with information for Ann, who would come up with the numbers, go back to the site, negotiate, and close the deal. Never will I forget the day that I loaded the computer and went many miles from Little Rock to visit a prospect. Steps one and two had gone fine. Then came the problem. Horrors! The computer would not boot! Nightmare of nightmares! Steps four and following certainly would not take place if I could not execute step three! The only saving grace was that I had gone early to set up the system, and no one else was in the room. Thank heavens our wonderful technician was in the office back home. I became hands for his brain, trying this and then that and then the other. Finally, something worked, and the demo was able to proceed smoothly. I wish I could report an immediate sale to that clinic—not so, until many years after this event.

That incident reminds me of another several years later. I had flown to Corpus Christi, Texas, to demo the system not to the office manager and staff but rather to the *doctors* and to—oh, woe—their *consultant*. We were to meet at the country club and have a light sandwich dinner before the demo and discussion. All of that sounded like a fine plan, and all proceeded normally. I even checked out the equipment ahead of time. However, biting down on the sandwich, I felt a crunch. So many thoughts pass through one's mind at times such as this. "It is something that should not be there, but what is it? Do I want to know or not?"

It took but a moment for me to figure it out: the gold crown from one of my teeth. Then the immediate worry was the amount of pain that might or might not occur within the next several minutes. Would I be able to do the demo and have the discussion afterward? This story had a happier ending than the first story. I was able to extract the crown unobtrusively and spirit it into my pocket. There was little to no pain involved, the demo proceeded smoothly, and this group became our client and remained so for years.

In further reviewing the calendar, I have been able to reconnect with the emotions I felt at the time. It was great fun to make the sales, to fly or drive to far-flung locations, and to have meetings and hold training sessions in posh corporate suites in Houston, Dallas and Denver. However, there are other notations just as important to my happiness at the time. Undoubtedly, Ann can list similar ones from her own experiences.

"Grass seed"—"J.D. Bennett Air Conditioner Service"—"pick up cleaning"—"windshield"—"dog food"—"dentist"—and similar notes reminded me that I was responsible for running the household. I once heard some very sage advice, "If it's to be, it's up to me." That was it. If the windshield got fixed, the dentist appointment scheduled, or the dog food purchased, it was up to me to do it. If there seem to be overtones of implied martyrdom there, I don't mean it to be that way. No, instead I look back and feel thankful. Thankful that God had provided me with a wonderful home and lovely piece of property—and that the house-that-periodically-had-to-be-cleaned wasn't any larger than it was. Also, I remember leaning back after paying bills and being so thankful that God had provided us with a thriving business that would allow me to pay all that was owed.

Other notations indicate that I did take time to have lunch with friends, but not often enough. There is no reason to regret, but I am now trying to make sure that I include time for friends by contacting them by e-mail, letter, phone call, or in person—or preferably a combination of one or more.

"Piano lesson"—"teacher conference"—"hair cuts"—"fish tank"—"Nutcracker"—"tennis lesson"—"summer camp information"—"talent show"—"portrait studio"—"school carnival"—"buy goodies"—"cut pumpkin." These are the notes that brought the greatest warmth to my heart and moisture to my eyes. A few years before, Penn and I had watched a *Sesame Street* episode describing families. It emphasized that a family didn't always consist of a mother, a father, and one or more children. No, it could be grandmother-father-child, aunt-mother-children, grandparents-child, any number of other combinations—even mother-child. That one described us—we were a family, albeit a tiny one. Despite the busy schedules, we were very close. Even with love and support from friends and family, at that time in our lives, when we got right down to it, we were living another Helen Reddy song, "You and Me Against the World." Even at Penn's young age, we had to depend upon each other for many things.

Then that summer provided me with an opportunity to test my maturity: Penn wanted to attend a summer camp for a whole week. Previously she had spent days at a time with one or the other grandmother or her aunt and uncle. Those were all family—this was different. Hot Springs really isn't too far from Little Rock, unless you are taking your only child to leave her there for a week. I survived, and she thrived. In fact, she told me later that that week had ended up being such an important one in her life. Neither of us will forget the closing assembly. (The time for me to go down and retrieve her had finally arrived!) Miss Nettie said, "Now boys and girls, we have had a lot of fun activities here at camp. When you go back home, I don't want any of you to be heard saying that you are *bored*. Remember that only *boring* people get *bored*." This was an important week for me, as well.

Since by the latter part of 1986 the MOMS theme was changing from "freight train going so fast" to songwriter Chantal Kreviazuk's "I'm leaving on a jet plane," I treasured the time shared with Penn and ached when we were apart, especially when my absence coincided with some special event. At first Penn could only see the negative side of my being away. However, it really didn't take her long to figure out that there also were positives. For one, Mother (her Mama S.) came frequently with my absences. Not a bad deal having an adoring, loving grandmother at one's beck and call. Also, Penn soon realized that plane trips meant frequent flyer miles and that they could eventually be converted to tickets...for the two of us to go to Hawaii and the Caribbean. "Aren't you going any place this week, Mom?"

"No, but soon we will fly again to Las Vegas for—you guessed it, COMDEX!"

FAMILIES

13

Ann speaks:

It was the beginning of 1987, and we had just moved into our new business offices. Even though we had operated for the last year out of the old retail location, the physical move to a professional setting was going to prove to the world that Susan and I were serious about our new change. The move provided an outward expression of a newly formed inward goal.

In 1986 we had adopted the name Medical Office Management Systems along with our old name, Computer Systems Integrators (MOMS/CSI). It was now possible to change our logo completely to reflect our newfound industry. We had also begun to print a newsletter to send to our clients announcing helpful information and upcoming events. One of those events was the Grand Reopening of MOMS/CSI on January 30. Once we had established this connection, the business world would be aware of our happenings. The Greater Little Rock Chamber of Commerce attended our Grand Reopening, and we were entertained by the Catholic High School band and some prominent politicians. We had a very good turnout, quite different from the grand opening in our retail location in 1984. We were now representing small businesses, and doctors were part of this environment.

In addition to our Grand Reopening, we began an inward shift in our business to reflect our new business philosophy, which included establishing separate departments and setting up a true business infrastructure. At this point, we had given little attention to our business organization, other than in marketing and getting new installations. As our number of employees grew, we needed to concentrate on building up the business from the inside out and establishing an efficient operation.

When we were in Japan in 1984, we had been fascinated by the Japanese style of management and their ability to foster long-term work relationships. This was exactly what we wanted to do. Their culture included treating everyone like family and allowing feedback from all employees. We began to adopt this philosophy within our own business. This process has been called Total Quality Management, and its roots are from the Japanese business environment. The Japanese also stressed continuing to improve daily on all activities to keep the benchmarks going steadily upward. Unfortunately, the Japanese culture has fallen victim to the demands of westernization, and it is my personal opinion that this has served as its downfall. The pressure of becoming global and the movement toward everything getting larger can also add to the inability to work as a family environment.

We set up specific departments and chose leaders to head each department. Even though we only had four departments at the time, it was a good start. It provided a clear indication of who was in charge and set the stage for team-building concepts which are still very popular today. Each member of the team was given the flexibility to suggest and submit new ideas, but the department head of the team had final decision-making power. Of course it goes without saying that Susan and I had final say-so. We learned some very valuable lessons during that time, and one of the most valuable was to never say "no" unless you have to, because that way it means more when you do. I have often said that managing is like parenting. I believe there are many similarities. Basic respect that is earned and freedom to open the doors to creativity are essential in both families and businesses. If leaders and parents only say "no" when necessary, no one's spirit or confidence is broken. I have also found that expecting employees to live up to the potential you see in them is an excellent way to achieve the desired results. Very seldom do people fail to live up to expectations placed on them if the expectations are based on sincerity and represent the best interest of the cause, or in this case the department, they represent.

We were very fortunate to have some wonderful young people seek our company for employment. We tried to make our office a fun place to work to foster long-term relationships. Everyone was expected to work hard, and the company represented the end that we were all seeking to improve. It was understood that when the company succeeded, we all succeeded. Although our hiring skills needed improving, God was always faithful to provide us quality individuals. Those who were not team oriented never seemed to last very long. In 1987, we rewarded the best manager for a given period with a trip to New Orleans, and this became a tradition that we carried out for many years.

We began to use our newsletter to introduce special marketing programs and to announce special items of interest to our clients. The newsletter also provided an avenue to feature clinics and print testimonials when they were offered. We printed in our newsletter that Susan and I had won a ski trip to Vail, Colorado, for having sold the most Wallaby packages in a given time frame. One might expect that there would be discontent among the employees for our having won the trip, but I honestly never heard of any complaints in this area. Susan also stated in a newsletter during that time that "both the strengths and weaknesses of a person become glaringly obvious when he or she is called to rise to any occasion. In the MOMS company, there is a lot of strength." We had begun to spot real talent and true character in our employees, and we wanted to reinforce these attributes as often as we could. This continued support through positive efforts could produce miracles.

We also used the newsletter to announce the number of systems we had sold, and in July we delivered our fiftieth system in grand style to a doctor in Texarkana, Arkansas. We rented a limousine to deliver it, and the doctor went along with the celebration by having his entire staff as part of the ceremony. His young son was also present and got a ride in the limousine. People seemed to enjoy being a part of doing fun things like this, so we would pull out all the stops when the occasion merited. Since we all worked very hard, this was a welcome respite from our fast-paced schedule and provided the balance we all needed.

In the fall, we planned a Users' meeting. The first Users' meetings were held in our facility. We also started scheduling in-house training classes for office managers. We always made it a point to train on-site for all the basics, but additional issues came up after the system had been used for a while, and the additional classes were extremely helpful. This was also a wonderful form of advertising and helped build a strong network of loyal customers. Even back in those days, employee turnover did occur, and there was always new personnel to be trained. We offered classes based on these needs.

By the end of 1987, we had computerized seventy-five physicians' offices. We could hardly believe it. That might not sound impressive to many, but most of these systems were sold one at a time. I was involved in selling many of them, but by then we had a wonderful salesperson who had stepped up to the plate and continued to add to our numbers. Even though I always enjoyed selling, it was far more rewarding to teach others to do the same thing. I was now enjoying much more success through others than from my single efforts. I felt a great deal of pride when I looked around at the bright shining faces of those wonderful employees that were a part of the MOMS organization. Being the oldest member of the team, I likened the feeling to that of being a parent again.

Just as I was enjoying being a parent in an extended family, nothing prepared me for the pride I would feel in January of 1988 when my daughter, Beverly, became the mother of my first grandchild, Jordan. This young man made his appearance on January 25 and weighed an even ten pounds! Since my daughter lived in Dallas, I was on the first plane to be there as close to the delivery as possible. My only regret was that her father was unable to participate in this wonderful event. My daughter shared with me later that she felt the tears of joy from her dad during the time her son was born. This provided a comfort to her for many years to come. God is faithful to give us exactly what we need, when He determines we need it. All He wants from us is to give him the credit for His gift.

In January of this same year, we were featured in an article in the business section of the *Arkansas Gazette*. The article stated, "Competition among doctors and the sea of federal paperwork has meant big business for a company founded by two Arkansas women." The writer printed a background sketch of the history of the company and brief biographical profiles on each of us. I was quoted as saying, "MOMS wishes to take this opportunity to thank our customers, who have been so instrumental in making this success possible. We continue to search for more and more ways to serve you better. As a result, 1988 is going to be an exciting year for all of us."

When 1988 began, it was filled with hopeful anticipation. We lost two of our valued employees due to circumstances beyond our control, and others stepped in to fill their spots. In all of the years I was in business, it always hurt to lose an employee. It was probably not professional of me, but I got attached to our employees. Just as a mother has to let go of her children, a manager has to let go of employees. We were building a reputation, and more and more candidates were seeking out our company for employment. The former employees were still in our hearts, but we had to fill those slots with qualified people who could serve our customers. We appreciated the efforts each employee had made and used their work as a building block for others who followed.

This same year, we installed another out-of-state clinic, in Columbus, Ohio. By that time, AT&T had decided that their expertise level was not as great as they had hoped, and they began looking for resellers who were qualified to take over their installations. They had managed to sell a lot of hardware (not unlike selling their telephones), but when it came to having the technical expertise for training and support, they just couldn't seem to hit the mark. We had learned early in our business through trial and error that industry knowledge was vital in servicing customers. The saying that it "takes one to know one," is certainly true. We thought like doctors, and many of our personnel had worked in clinics and understood the medical environment, as well. Because of this, we "adopted" several clinics through the years, and we were very happy to get them. It broadened our scope, and we were quickly increasing our local status to one of a regional company.

As Susan mentioned earlier, we were fortunate to be awarded a large state contract to computerize the Area Health Education Centers in Arkansas. This was the largest contract we sold, and it required purchasing a "performance bond." This project was greatly enhanced by the expertise of our newly promoted training director. Susan was able to delegate some of the responsibility to this young woman. Another woman we had promoted to Director of Support helped build our application support staff into a very skilled and talented group.

We constantly tried to increase the staff's knowledge by setting up an in-house certification process. Also, several employees went to New Jersey for training on the system and became certified trainers.

We made a quick trip to COMDEX that year, but it was mostly to make contacts with the other resellers and to see if there were any enhancements we could find. We wanted to visit several booths because they had software that complemented our medical package. We had begun receiving inquiries about word processing capabilities and other applications that could augment and streamline the efficiency of our clients. We always tried to stay ahead of the curve in our field, and getting out of the office proved helpful in stretching ourselves and seeing what people were doing in other parts of the country. A business owner can easily become so tied to her business that she can easily get stale and not realize what is going on elsewhere. This is why we continued to attend selected national conventions targeted to our industry.

On January 7, 1989, I became a grandmother again. Stephanie Anne Baskette weighing in at seven pounds and five ounces was born in Dayton, Ohio, to parents Brad and Sherry. Once again, I was on the first available plane to arrive quickly after the delivery. Even though they were planning to visit Arkansas in February, I could not pass up the opportunity to share in this miraculous event. God gives us a glimpse into the future when we gaze into the eyes of a child. Where were the years going? They were slipping away. It had been two and a half years since I had attended their wedding. It seemed like only a few months.

Soon after my return from visiting my family, an event occurred which was another milestone in our company. On Friday, January 27,

MOMS delivered its one-hundredth system to a large pulmonary clinic in Little Rock. It was delivered not only in a limousine, but with a chauffeur as well. The limousine arrived at the MOMS offices to transport individuals and computer system to the site. Two key members of the clinic staff were on hand to welcome the entourage and to receive a balloon bouquet and certificate of recognition from the MOMS staff. By this time, we had added a couple more very talented employees. We were certainly going to need them to keep up with our exploding business.

In March of that year, one of our most valuable employees gave birth to her first child, a boy. We added something new to our employee policy: maternity leave. Fortunately, the mother returned as soon as she was able and worked for us for many years. Experiences like this allowed us to become more and more involved in the personal lives of our employees.

Employees are the most valuable part of a business, and if they are not well cared for, they will leave to seek other opportunities. In the many management classes I attended, I learned that the number one reason an employee stays with an organization is appreciation. Of course, salary and benefits are important, but an environment that is satisfying and produces a general feeling of acceptance is critical in keeping long-term employees. After all, employees spend approximately one-third of their lives in a working environment; why shouldn't they work where they feel important? This is a fringe benefit that a small business can provide better than a large corporation that cannot devote the time to get to know all its employees on a first name basis. For this reason, many people prefer to work in a smaller, more intimate setting.

In the fall, we hosted the largest Users' meeting we had ever had. It was held at a local hotel, and over one hundred people attended. We offered door prizes to lucky attendees who had to be present to win. (This prevented people from leaving the meeting early in the day.) We provided guest speakers from the medical industry, and clinics were divided into groups of like specialty for workshops. This resulted in great networking and knowledge sharing. By then we had 125 installations, and we were looking forward to the new year with great anticipation. We were really beginning to make a mark in the medical industry and were becoming known throughout the country. God had truly been good to us. He was also providing us with many opportunities to reach out to others, and we received more than just material success from our business. The business had truly become an outgrowth of our former THEOS ministry. Once again, we felt God's guidance along the path He had set for us.

As I reflect on the era of the 1980s, I am truly thankful that we had an Advocate on our side, considering the many mistakes and blunders that we made due to inexperience. Fortunately none of the mistakes proved to be irreversible. We had seen many computer companies who were "high rollers" in their time go out of business. We had also lost some of the really big deals to larger companies, and we lost the business of those who would never consider doing business with a woman. We always felt that God had a reason for those circumstances and trusted Him to give us guidance when we most needed it or when we earnestly sought His direction. We had made a commitment to Him that we would run an ethical business no matter what, and this sometimes meant less business in the short run. We felt we were going to be in the business for the long run or until God directed our paths differently. We were also provided an opportunity to sample the world's "sweet smell of success," and we were truly grateful. Humanly, we wondered if our skills and expertise were going to be enough to take us into the next decade with continued success. It remained to be seen if this was in God's will.

EDUCATION AND DELEGATION

14

Susan speaks:

Three articles from Volume V, Issue 1, of our newsletter *MOMS at Work* collectively and unknowingly presaged accurately the first five years of the 1990s for MOMS. One forecast the direction of the computer industry as a whole. Another, written by a physician-client, predicted the increasingly vital role of computers in the lives of not just physicians but all individuals. Finally, I included an essay describing an evolution taking place within MOMS corporately and within Ann and me individually.

The first issue of the 1990s stated, "MOMS has been around during just about all of the previous decade and has been able to watch the explosions and the ripples in the computer industry in general and the medical computer industry, specifically…What is ahead in the 1990s?…Indicators point toward faster, cheaper, more powerful machines with great storage potentials…Perhaps the surest prediction is that this industry will continue to barrel ahead." Even Roman augurs with their strange methods of prognostication could not have made a more accurate prophecy. During those years the computer industry, generally, and the medical computer industry, specifically, barreled forward, full steam ahead, no slowing down in sight. MOMS was there. By the beginning of the decade, we already had almost nine years of experience in this very field. We were right in the middle of this ground swell, running as fast as we could just to stay on top, or perhaps a little ahead, of it.

Back in 1982, while attending that very first Wallaby training session, I jotted down a quote, "The well-educated consumer is our best customer." Ann and I discovered that this maxim was so true and so important to our success that we should have had it tattooed on our foreheads, or at least on the palms of our hands. Dr. George Bohmfalk was one of our best customers for many reasons, including the fact that he stayed so well informed on issues related to computers and medical computing. From the strength of his conviction that physicians should become better informed in this field, he wrote "Physician, Computerize Thyself" and subsequently allowed us to publish excerpts from the article in our newsletter. Dr. Bohmfalk underscored the way that many physicians were beginning to view "the computer" and the effects that "it" could have on their lives and practices. "Becoming computer-literate bears several similarities to learning medicine. It's challenging, precise, sometimes frustrating, often exciting, definitely rewarding. But whereas one might function perfectly well in the future without knowing medicine, the same cannot be said about computers." Initially skeptical of the true efficacy of computers, he had realized that he could not do without one. "The magic moment came during the demonstration of the office system. The representative (from MOMS) asked whether I might ever want or need to access information at the office from home...A home computer linked by modem to the office was the solution." A light bulb had come on. He could use this system at the office and at home. Dr. Bohmfalk did his homework with an open mind and, consequently, reaped the benefits. Ann and I were more convinced than ever of our responsibility to open this world to our doctors, yes, but also to all who worked with them. Education and training were the key.

My "back page" essay was entitled "How (Bitter)Sweet It Is!" I began by describing my feelings while watching an airplane pull away from the gate. "That time that airplane had my daughter, my only child, inside. For the first time she was taking a plane trip by herself! I had to relinquish control of her life to others." Ann and I had had a similar experience within the company not long before. From incorporation until February of 1990, we had "run everything." As MOMS had grown, developed, and expanded, more employees were needed for added efficiency and effectiveness, but we still directed all activities. Finally it had become evident that for the company to reach another stage of maturity we needed to redirect our daily activities toward specialized projects and begin to let go—to put more control of the life of our "baby" into the hands of others. We needed to allow others to direct daily operations. The promotion of two wonderful young women to the managerial ranks was not easy for us. They did well, but for several days Ann and I found ourselves "still arranging schedules and doing other tasks which we had supposedly handed over." Finally I was able to say, "We are getting better, and the company is stronger for it, just as my daughter is for having that first plane ride without me."

These two experiences accurately depicted other aspects of our next five years, corporately and personally. We knew we had to let go more and more. The "how" and "to whom" became the challenges. Personally, it was in this time frame that I had to loosen the apron strings more than at any time before or since. Undoubtedly, Ann and all mothers who read this have had parallel experiences and will recognize the emotions wrenched during these, the high school years. Similarly, all who have started businesses and watched them grow will identify.

At this time I was reminded of a talk presented during my own freshman year at Harpeth Hall School. It has become so evident during the many years since graduation that this wonderful school attempted to prepare me for all phases of life, not just the academic. This speech was given soon after an unmanned, sub-orbital space rocket had been launched from Cape Canaveral, as it was still known back then. Minutes before lift-off, the support tower backed away and the only remaining connection to the rocket was a device called, appropriately, an umbilical cord. The final action before lift-off was the severing of this connection.

The speaker said that he felt we were all mature enough to hear and understand his message. Just as it was necessary for the umbilical cord of the rocket to be removed before it could soar, the same is true of us in our relationships with our parents. At first each of us depends entirely on a parent for care and sustenance. A truly caring parent is one who makes himself or herself less and less essential as the child matures, so that at the time of the parent's death, assuming that it is timely, the child-as-adult is fully capable of living a happy and productive life without that parent. We were hoping to be able to apply this wisdom to the life of our company.

During the first half of the 1990s, computers, medicine and medical computing all were undergoing not just changes but *upheavals.* Frequently Ann and I would look at each other and ask why in the world we had chosen this dual industry, both parts of which were in such states of flux. We knew. We had experience; we had expertise; it was an exciting time to be right there. Wallaby was continuing to release updates to the medical software that would enable us to provide the needed features to our clients. A Credit and Collections module was added, and computerized UB82 insurance filing became a reality (a mixed blessing, with all of the resultant headaches). Since the handwriting on the wall clearly indicated that eventually all claims would need to be filed electronically, we entered the electronic data interchange early. A close relationship with Blue Cross/ Blue Shield, and especially with a competent woman named Patty Mask, helped to make us successful in this field from the outset. She not only helped us through some rough spots and acquiesced to speaking at our Users' group meetings but also was a constant source of encouragement in our endeavors.

As time went on, Ann and I were able to quote in truth another line from *Woman of the Year.* We "made the right decision again! Right? Right!" No matter how much we tried to remain openly thankful to the Lord for His allowing us this successful business and to give Him glory for His guidance, we lapsed too often into humanity, temporarily forgetting warning words from the Bible such as "puffed up." Admittedly, some incidents made us feel really proud of ourselves. One was a 1990 article by Phil Ellett from the *Computer Reseller News,* with the headline, "Dealers, VAR's must prepare for the UNIX wave." It continued, "The microcomputer marketplace is being swept up in an exciting fourth wave...UNIX/Xenix." How smug we felt, and undoubtedly looked, with the knowledge that we had installed our first UNIX system more than six years before—and this site was still our faithful client. Fortunately, we did recover our perspective by saying, "Lucky guess? We believe that it was more than that." We knew that it was more than that.

Simultaneously, the Wallaby medical software we had selected six years before was receiving positive press. In *MD Computing*, Dr. Matthew Cushing, Jr., complimented the system by saying, "Of all of the programs I have reviewed, The Resident [by Wallaby] remains the most flexible." (There was that word again!) He concluded, "This is an excellent program that has kept pace with the times." So there we were, with more than six years' experience with the UNIX operating system and the Wallaby medical software, both being touted as the best in the industry. We did feel blessed.

The article by Dr. Cushing was especially dear to our hearts since he verbalized the essence of our focus by saying, "…training and retraining are essential, as with any sophisticated software. For this you will need a top-quality dealer." By the mid-nineties, we knew that MOMS was definitely one of the top Wallaby dealers in the country. As proof that our personal opinion was buttressed by fact, Ann and I were both selected to sit on the very first Wallaby Dealer Council and attend its meeting in Mahwah, New Jersey. This and subsequent similar gatherings allowed us not only to obtain detailed information concerning the future of this company and its products but also to offer grass-roots input from the desires and needs of our clients. Even beyond, though, the meetings provided opportunities to forge relationships with people from literally all over the country. Some developed into important business alliances, others precious friendships.

As indicated before, the transition to a willingness to appoint people to middle management positions was at first very difficult for both Ann and me. Young, enthusiastic, diligent, and efficient, the two ladies we promoted showed us immediately that they were up to the task. The bonus for us was immense once we did let go. Finally, although still very busy, we were able to refocus our priorities as we had never been able to do before. Hopefully, just in time. It is my guess that few working mothers retrospectively wish they had spent more time at work and less with their children. Guilt often rears its ugly head, and certainly did for me. What a cliché but oh, so true: "Where did the time go?" Suddenly, Penn was a freshman in high school! How did that happen so soon?

Thankfully, a review of my calendar entries indicates that finally my life had become more balanced, and I was certainly more involved with her and with her activities. I won't go so far as to indulge in self-flagellation for past omissions, but it is evident how blessed I was by this redirection. Church, youth group, school retreat, school carnival, talent show, awards presentations, Summer Spree—memories of these have enhanced our relationship in the years since that time.

One summer she and others from her school were selected to attend a marine biology session off the coast of Florida. The only stipulation was that the students and the instructor had to be SCUBA certified. "Penn, are there any openings in the class? If so, would you mind if I became certified, too?" Fortunately, Penn didn't (as far as I know) go through the "I am so ashamed to be seen with my mom" stage and seemed pleased that I wanted to explore the underwater world with her. A great experience, even when I found myself bunking with the kids when we had to do our open-water testing!

Similarly, almost simultaneously Penn and I both became fascinated by the idea of going to Haiti with a group of teenagers and adults from our church. The purpose of the trip was to help build a dormitory for a Christian camp near Pignon. Even though my own mother was not at all taken with the idea, our enthusiasm grew and our plans continued on track—until the word from my doctor: surgery. It should be done soon, but there would not be time to recover before the trip. Apron strings—apron strings…it was all fine in my own mind knowing that Penn would go to a "third-world" country— but with me. "Now, do I let her go, anyway? I hadn't planned on that."

Faith, Susan, faith.

Returning to Little Rock with Haitian baskets and shirts and with hair braided into tiny "corn rows," Penn evidently would never be the same. This was a life-changing experience. How I wished more than ever that I could have been with her. The very next summer another opportunity opened, and we both jumped onto it immediately. For more than a week we U.S. kids and adults (or were we just older kids?) participated in a summer camp with Haitian kids and adults. Now I will never be the same. Penn understands that, and I understand the same about her. My letting go at MOMS and letting go of her continued to result in untold blessings.

Concurrently, Ann was thankful for more flexibility in planning her life. What a joyous time, the arrival of a grandchild. It doesn't matter how many there are; each is welcomed with happiness and thanksgiving. Grandchild number three, a little girl, precipitated an immediate trip to Ohio to see not only Melanie Elizabeth but also the mom, dad, and now "older sister." Besides, back in Little Rock grandson number one enjoyed the time that Grandma spent with him. She shouldn't work all the time!

My own family ties were strengthened in a way that I would never have predicted. Just as my brother Scottie is eight years older than I, Frank was eight years older than his sister Wilda. When Frank and I first started "dating" at age twelve, Wilda was truly the little sister—only four years old! Over the years she and I forged a very close friendship, which remained and even strengthened after Frank's death. By the early '90s this "little sister" had grown up, earned her law degree, and opened a brokerage office—and then became the financial advisor for MOMS. It all made me feel a little old but a lot proud.

As 1990 drew to a close, each of us at MOMS was continuing to become busier and busier, even with an excellent staff. A new territory opened when we signed a client in Des Moines, Iowa, our ninth state. Ann and I traveled to the Boston area to meet with Dragon, pioneers in the field of voice recognition. A lot was going on! In the midst of all of this, we began planning for 1991, the *tenth* Anniversary year for MOMS.

Two themes, indicative of both our past and our future, were designed for this anniversary year: "No Train; No Gain" and "Celebrating Successful Syntheses." The first went right along with Dr. Cushing's article mentioning the importance of training and retraining. We took that to heart and scheduled classes not only in Little Rock but also in Hot Springs, Kentucky, and Tennessee. Wherever we saw a concentrated need, we took our show on the road. Now just as I was saying that our managers alleviated a lot of our time pressure, I realize that the growth of our business meant that we were all still making time sacrifices. Ann's was mainly for marketing and mine for training. For example, January 1991 was a killer: January 2-3, I was in Springfield; 5-10 in Tennessee and Kentucky; 13-17 in Des Moines and Springfield; 24 in Springfield; and 27-29 in Chicago. Training was important!

Our second theme was "Celebrating Successful Syntheses."

- Celebrating: "commemorating with ceremony or festivity."
- Successful: "coming about…or turning out to be as was hoped for."
- Syntheses: "the putting together of parts…so as to form a whole."

In 1991 we did just that—"commemorated with festivity" the fact that MOMS, by "putting together parts to form a whole," had "turned out to be as was hoped for." Well, to tell the truth, MOMS at ten had far surpassed any hope that I had ever had for her. It was time to celebrate the MOMS milestone.

May 14, 1991, Chenal Country Club. "Ann, did it seem like just yesterday, instead of ten years ago, when we were in the lawyer's office signing the Articles of Incorporation?" There we were, though, surrounded by our nine employees. Special pride filled Ann's heart since one of the nine was her daughter, Beverly. I was thrilled since my two most special people, daughter Penn and mother, Dorothea Sudduth, were celebrating with us. Furthermore, our continuing close association with Wallaby Corporation was evidenced by the fact that one of the four principals of the company took the time and made the effort to come to Little Rock for our event. A great time truly was had by all.

A final note related to these recollections comes from my "back-page" essay from the anniversary edition of our newsletter:

Even though…the word "synthesis" is derived from the Greek words meaning "with" and "to place," it became patently clear that another significance for MOMS is embedded within this word. From the Greek language, "syn" does denote "with"; however, "the" often signifies the word "theos" or "god." In this case, I like to be reminded that MOMS was founded through a firm belief that God was leading the formation and development of this company, a true "syn-the"-sis, a "God-with"-ness. We will strive in this anniversary year and beyond, to stay "with God" in all of our decisions and endeavors.

With the party behind us and knowing what was ahead of us in the fall, Ann and I decided to take a brief trip to Colorado to clear the cobwebs. Any visit any time of the year to the Aspen/Snowmass area is about as close to heaven for me as any place on earth. This time we decided to push that analogy a little further by signing up for a pre-dawn balloon ride. The night before, Ann (who tends not to do well in anything that even *might* produce motion-sickness) was just about to change her mind and was thinking of any excuse why she should not go. Knowing that she undoubtedly would enjoy the experience if she did go and having been in business with her for ten years, I knew exactly what to say. "Well, that is just fine if you really do not want to go...just remember that the tickets have already been paid for!" Of course, that did it—and she had a grand time. It did take nearly fifteen minutes after we landed to pry her white knuckles off the balloon cables, but she did have fun. A wonderful tradition among balloonists is that no matter how early the hour, a successful flight is toasted with champagne. This she did not refuse!

Yes, the fall was especially busy since growth had meant outgrowth—of the office space—and the need for a move. We were tired of having offices on two different floors. Besides, our training room was no longer large enough. Like hermit crabs, we shed our old home and moved into a larger one. Despite the joy of a big classroom, open support areas, and lovely offices, it was still a time-consuming hassle to make the move; but it was definitely worth it. One of the most frequent staff comments we heard was, "Now we have a sink—and running water! No more going to the restrooms for water for coffee!!"

We truly were busy. But so often in the midst of our most intense busyness, God shows us a little surprise snapshot which He uses to make us stop, breathe, slow down, and think. One day He used a wrong turn for His purpose. The sun was more than an hour from its daily appearance when I headed toward Paragould, Arkansas, for a client meeting. Evidently on autopilot, my Maxima turned west instead of east at the Interstate intersection and continued toward the next city to the west. I suddenly came to my senses and grabbed a state map. "Silly, Paragould is up *there*, the *northeast* part of the state, and you are heading west!" As luck would have it, I was approaching an exit for the west-to-east state highway that intersects with the one that I should have been on originally. Beating myself up for wasting so much time so unnecessarily, I came upon a scene now indelibly etched into my mind, and immediately removed my foot from the accelerator. Day was breaking, mist still rising from fields surrounding a small brick rural school building. Out front was a flag pole with the standard already on high. With locked hands and bowed heads there stood a circle of students. "See you at the pole!" had undoubtedly been their salutation the day before. No law had been broken; they were worshiping freely and openly, silently and early. Once again God was telling me to slow down, and to focus first on the highest priorities of life, including taking time to worship Him.

In keeping with a desire to prioritize corporate activities, Ann and I tried to set aside a significant amount of time and effort to implement an annual event that became one of our most important corporate functions. Even though our new training room was large, it would still not accommodate our vastly popular Users' Group Meetings. We had been having these for a number of years, changing location with the number of participants. By this time we had already gone from one tiny meeting room at a local hotel to a single banquet room and then to a double one. Having maximized that facility, we moved to a huge room at one of the hospitals. With their audiovisual equipment, this room was perfect. It was high time for the group to have a name. The obvious became the embraced: MOMS Users' Group Meeting, or MUG for short. Perfect—it was easy to say and favors from that year forward were a given: mugs.

It didn't stop—it didn't stop. By July of 1992 the number of MOMS clients in the Springfield, Missouri, area was putting a strain on not only the training staff but on our families as well. The wonderful husband of one of our trainers became a "Mr. Mom" personified to their two precious boys. He would make sure that our trainer always had pictures of the boys so she wouldn't forget what they looked like. With happy families as one of our highest priorities, Ann and I finally admitted that it was time to establish a local presence, for the good of both the Springfield clients and the preservation of staff members' marriages. Another leap: our first out-of-state employee! The one who arrived on our doorstep was certainly a godsend. She not only was pleasant and outgoing but also already knew the system.

Explosion of business in this area could be attributed in part to our being awarded another multi-site contract, this one with St. John's Hospital. A new concept was developing within the field of medicine. Hospitals were starting to buy medical practices. Accustomed to independent, almost entrepreneurial physicians, at first it seemed strange to think of their being willing to sell their practices and become mere employees of a larger corporation. The times, they truly were a-changin'. Despite trepidation at the final outcome of such an arrangement, we knew well the mounting pressures faced by our physician clients. Reimbursements were being cut as HMOs were bursting onto the scene with promises, promises, promises. Maybe this would be a sensible alternative. At least we knew that we would be able to fulfill all they needed from us. As practices were purchased, we were called to install, train, and support a computer billing system for each. This was a wonderful plan for us. We just hoped it would be the same for the providers.

Meanwhile both our technical and application support staffs in Little Rock were becoming busier and busier. We handled well over a thousand calls each month. As more and more sales were made, the installation group was being taxed, and the trainers were going full tilt. The strain was beginning to show. Customer complaints crept in, calls were not being returned promptly, and frustrations arose on all sides. To make matters worse, the medical industry itself was experiencing even more turmoil with the onset of new insurance forms, new Medicare codes and coding procedures, and new reporting requirements. We were right in the middle of all of this and tried desperately to impress upon our clients that we were all in the same boat, bailing as fast as we could, and that it would take cooperation from all sides to weather this storm. Yes, we did have our problems; we were understaffed for the load. There was only one solution: eleven, twelve, fifteen, then eighteen employees—and all of them needed. With all of us pulling together and staying in touch with our clients, we were able to regain control of the ship and put it back on course.

It was perfect timing, since in winter of 1992 we received an RFP (Request for Proposal) from EPIC Healthcare, Dallas. Perusing the lengthy request form, Ann and I realized that MOMS could, indeed, handle such a project. It was one (albeit sizable) step beyond the Springfield venture in that EPIC owned many hospitals, not just one. Each of these was in the process of purchasing medical practices, and billing offices were being set up to service them. If we could do St. John's, we could do EPIC. Our written response to the request was more than an inch thick. The time spent generating this document and flying to Dallas for an arduous "show me" session was abundantly rewarded since our proposal was the one accepted. The good news brought out the poet in my daughter as she posted the following on a fluorescent green poster board:

You are awesome, You are great—
Now it's time to celebrate!
I would have written you an EPIC length poem,
But my brain fried,

I Love You!
Penn
Philippians 4:4

We were fortunate that we had reinforced our staff before the awarding of this contract since the sites to be serviced were far flung, from California to Texas to Florida to, yes, even Springfield, Missouri. Not wanting to impose drastically on the other members of the training team, I was a self-sacrificing leader. As I indicated in our newsletter with a description of our first EPIC installation at Clearwater Beach, Florida, "Two weeks there, staying at a room right on the beach—I know, tough assignment, but 'somebody had to do it.'" The same was true for the site in the middle of the Sonoma Valley, California—so far away!!! All of us were able to travel to some interesting places and meet more fascinating people, but it was hard work, really hard work.

By this time, the entire MOMS family had become very close. Just like a biological family, we shared the joys of birthdays, babies, puppies, and promotions, as well as the sorrows of deaths and disappointments. December 1992 brought to MOMS an event never duplicated. Several days before our scheduled annual Christmas Potluck, two of our employees came to talk with Ann and me. Since we knew they had been dating, it was no surprise when they told us they wanted to be married. "At the Christmas Potluck?!" How thrilled we were to realize the depth of the feelings our employees had for each other. They wanted to be married right there, among the people who meant the most to them.

We were the only four who knew. The normal food and fun proceeded as it had in years past. Just before everyone was to shift from main course to dessert, we asked one of the employees to take a card from the tree and read it. "You are invited to attend the wedding—*ooooooo*—of (these two employees)—*aaaaaahhhhhh*—on December (whatever it was)—*that's today*—at 1:00—*that's right now*!" Suddenly, the training room was transformed into a wedding chapel. Tables were moved and chairs aligned. Yards of computer paper formed the aisle. The Justice of the Peace arrived. We brought out the bouquet and boutonniere from Ann's office. Music? "I just happen to have my keyboard down in the car and even know how to play the 'Wedding March.'" Perfect!

Happy bride and groom! Purely by coincidence, one person who had been in charge of bringing dessert brought a white cake with white icing! I am still not sure how our wonderful cleaning lady felt about rice all over the office, but knowing her, she was more happy for the couple than miffed at having to do a little extra work. Being the magnanimous people that we are, Ann and I even allowed the couple to leave work two-and-a-half hours early!

Evidently, the efforts of the MOMS group were being recognized not just regionally, but also nationally. In 1992 the magazine *VAR Business* named our company as one of its "100+ Resellers of Distinction." Specifically, we were one of ten designated in the category "Innovative VARs." (VAR stands for Value Added Reseller.)In the accompanying article Ann was quoted as saying: "I've learned we have a lot of ability and energy within ourselves, and until we're put in a position of having to use it, sometimes it lies dormant." The article concludes, "Through their trials and tribulations, these women have made a name for themselves as more than mothers. They are MOMS."

We were truly honored, not only by this kind recognition but also for being nominated—then named as a finalist—in the *Arkansas Business* "Business of the Year, Category I" competition. (Categories are based on the number of employees.) A photographer had visited the offices of all of the finalists. What fun it was to see our own people at our own office projected up there on the huge screen of the banquet hall. It made us feel once again like proud MOMS. We were also proud moms, as Ann's Beverly and my Penn were at our table, along with my very own mom. (That made her a MOMS mom's mom?)

From the *MOMS at Work* newsletter: "Former Governor Frank White's wonderful voice boomed (as the ten of us around the table dared not or could not breathe). 'And the envelope please...Medical Office...!!!' That's all that we had to hear...It was one of those few moments in life that erupts with an exuberant, heart-felt, from the toes 'YES!!!!!!!!!!!!' Smiles, tears, hugs, hand-shakes, and high-fives!!"

What an honor—what a responsibility... "to maintain our standards of ethics, to increase our commitments to impeccable service, to have even more impact on the community, to provide even more secure and profitable positions for the employees and their families, to encourage others who are contemplating similar paths, and to give the glory to our God." It was exhilarating but heavy at the same time.

In the months of 1993 following the award ceremony, the beat went on. Changes seemed to hit us from all sides. Ann wrote, "As of June 30, 1993, Medicaid of Arkansas will no longer be accepting paper claims. [They] must be sent electronically...change...is here and here to stay, but...we at MOMS are committed to meeting these changes..." Fortunately, this was one of the changes predicted and prepared for by MOMS. Would that our crystal ball had worked so well on all of the others.

One transition within my personal life blessedly coincided with one of the busiest periods of my professional career. Between fall of 1993 and spring of 1994, the neat stack of boarding pass stubs on my bureau grew and grew. For a while I was spending many more nights in hotel rooms than in my own bed. Friday evening usually found me in D/FW or Love Field changing planes from somewhere, trying to get to Little Rock before the weekend began. Our EPIC contract was the main reason for this extensive travel. Exhausting, yes, but a real blessing.

From the newsletter: "In mid-September I watched a little girl (to mothers, even an eighteen-year-old is a little girl) walk away, away from me, away from the van that we had rented at the airport, away from her childhood...toward the Dartmouth campus...straight into her new life...How far is New Hampshire from Arkansas? Not far, as the heart flies."

These months of intense travel were also the first months of Penn's freshman year in college, of my being the only human in our home. By the time this schedule abated, I was getting really tired of the routine and even somewhat accustomed to being at home alone. No, not alone—Schnauzer Sam and kitties Sara Cat and Humuhumunukunukuapuaa (nicknamed G.C., or Grand Chat, French for Big Cat) provided great comfort, solace, and joy.

How proud the entire MOMS family was during that year when Ann was named as a member of the Greater Little Rock Leadership Institute, sponsored by the Greater Little Rock Chamber of Commerce. With competition fierce and the applications many, selection into this group is most decidedly a prestigious honor.

As 1993, "the year of change," had come to close, Ann and I predicted that 1994 would be not another year of change, but rather one of stretching. We wanted not only to stretch ourselves and our horizons but also to encourage our clients to do the same. Our desires were aimed toward higher degrees of efficiency and knowledge. Fortunately, we were not depending upon our soothsayer proficiencies for our livelihoods. (As a point of review—at that time Wallaby systems were our "bread and butter," and EPIC was our largest client.) The very first week of 1994, the year we had predicted would be one of "not so many changes," brought big news: first, Wallaby Software Corporation had been purchased by and merged with Physicians Computer Network, and second, EPIC had been purchased by HealthTrust (which was later bought by Columbia, which had previously purchased HCA, from which HealthTrust had spun off originally).

So much for our prognostications. Rather than bucking the trend, we went with the flow. We devised a new logo, a new corporate color,and a new look and name for the newsletter. *MOMS at Work* became *News from the Heart.* We were changing but stretching at the same time. No longer would one floor at Executive Court hold us. We had to stretch out onto the second as well.

What a half-decade it was! The ups, the downs; the successes, the failures; the problems, the solutions; the tears, the smiles; the admonitions, the praises; the expansion, the expansion, the expansion, the expansion. What next?

FROM DREAM
TO REALITY

15

Ann speaks:

The year 1995 was just beginning, and we knew that changes were on the horizon. As Susan mentioned, Wallaby was purchased by Physicians Computer Network. Wallaby had been an independent company, and PCN was a large corporation. We had no idea how this would affect our business and what changes it would necessitate. We did realize that we would need to continue our growth pattern and become a more formidable force in the industry if we were going to survive.

It is important to note that the business climate in general was beginning to place more emphasis on larger companies, and a few acquisitions were beginning to take place. Companies were also forming alliances with other companies in order to take advantage of economies of scale. We began strategizing about what our next moves should be and attended several business seminars in order to keep up with the latest trends in business and their impacts upon existing businesses. I feel compelled to point out once again how important it is with any size business to keep up with national trends. Changes in trends and in our economies greatly affect any business, regardless of its size.

We also continued our effort to delegate some of our lesser duties to others who were equally qualified. We found we were spending many hours of the day doing administrative things that were really not necessary, thus limiting our time to be creative. Now that the business was running smoothly, we needed to devote our time to developing business strategies. Once we changed our mode of thinking, we knew that new opportunities of thought and action would take place.

We had been able to computerize over two hundred clinics and become visible in eleven states. We had a choice at that point of continuing on this success track or exploring new strategies that could serve to help our business grow more quickly. We had been able to adopt over eighty clinics in Tennessee because the reseller, Blue Cross, no longer had an interest in reselling the product. Because we had developed a relationship working with them in the electronic claims part of their business, they personally recommended us to their customers. While this endorsement helped, we also had to sell ourselves to these customers. We put together a "Road Show" for as many of the customers as we could by setting up seminars and hosting some free training. After that, the support contracts began trickling in until we had picked up almost all of the clinics. It is also important to note that other competitors in the area were competing for this same business.

Later that same year, PCN bought a competitive software company and made it a subsidiary corporation. A dealer for that software was located just a few miles away from our location, right across the river. Since it was a small dealer, it occurred to us that we might try to discuss with the owner the possibility of combining our organizations. That way we could eliminate each other's competition and have many upgrades in the process. We were successful in a true meeting of the minds, and our first acquisition was completed by the end of the year, making it official on January 1, 1996. We received an added benefit in acquiring some extremely talented employees. Good technical employees with a thorough understanding of our industry are extremely valuable. We attended a meeting in Florida soon after that to discuss details of how PCN's owning both corporations would affect the dealer network. Our acquisition had put us in a good strategic position, since we now represented both companies' software packages.

Now that we had added an additional forty clinics and a number of employees to the MOMS network, we had to move to a facility that afforded more office space. We started out occupying most of the third floor of the building and later in the year we added some additional space on the second floor. During that time frame, we added a Research and Development department and began to develop new services such as electronic statements, interfaces to hospitals, and other customer programming services. There never seemed to be an end to opportunities to continue improving the efficiency of our clients. Also, technology demands were increasing, and our customers wanted to share in new ways to utilize their systems. Managed care demanded more capability of the systems, and more reports had to be designed to meet these needs. The industry was also changing the reimbursement doctors were receiving. Many of them wanted to be paid on their own productivity if they belonged to a group with several doctors. This created more programming needs and revenue opportunities. The R & D department was fast becoming one of our busiest departments.

Another trend emerged: reshuffling of the dealer network. Smaller dealers were no longer able to survive, and we began seeing a real shakeout in this year and the years to follow. We were also bursting at the seams despite our second and third floor rental spaces. We began to ask ourselves, "Is it time to look into moving to our own facility?" After a meeting with our accountant, it became clear to us that we were spending more rent each month than we would pay on a mortgage. At least with a mortgage, we would be building equity. We began to seriously consider owning our own building. We had learned not to sign long leases because our business requirements were constantly changing. Our lease would be up for renewal soon, and we looked forward to moving one last time. Our employees had spent many hours changing their work cubicles through the years; we knew they would be excited to learn of our plans. The announcement would be made when we felt it was appropriate, after all the details had been worked out.

In February of 1997, Susan and I were awarded a dealer trip to Palm Springs, California, because we were one of the top dealers in the country in sales and overall size. It was a wonderful trip and afforded a few days of rest and relaxation before we had to get back into the rat race. Not long after that we traveled to Florida to attend a VAR conference. These conferences offered us the same opportunity to meet with our peers as the COMDEX conventions had once provided.

In March, we made the announcement to our staff that MOMS had decided to build its own building and that we would work toward occupying it before the year's end. This was a tall order since we had not yet even located the property. Once again we painted an image in our minds and worried less about how we were going to accomplish it. We knew that exactly the right parcel would become available to us and that all it would take was hard work. Susan and I were used to that by now. Nothing had come easily to us in business, yet we had always been able to achieve our goals if we planted them firmly in our minds. This had become a process we had utilized as our business skills increased and our confidence level grew in proportion to our experience.

After an exhaustive search, we truly did find just the right piece of property in the western part of the city. It was in an area that was just beginning to grow in popularity. Once again we visited the planning commission and studied the growth patterns of the city to determine future trends. We also liked being ahead of the curve and not waiting until everything was in place. Susan and I felt this property, with its one and one-half acres, would provide not only the space we needed for a building, but also a great environment for our employees. Beautiful mountains surrounded the area that had been part of a large pasture in earlier times. Already a strip shopping center was being built, and another building was located within close proximity to our land. As an added bonus, it was located within just a few minutes of both our homes. We would not miss the busy traffic that posed a daily obstacle to our present location.

Despite the fact that I had become known as a pretty shrewd negotiator, I must admit that I had to utilize all my acquired expertise to arbitrate on a fair price for the property. It did not hurt that we negotiated the deal with a former landlord of ours from when we first started out in business. He really took a personal interest in us and sincerely wanted us to become landowners in the business tract that he managed. The next step was to find an architect that we felt comfortable with and plan the future MOMS building. We were successful in doing this and spent a great deal of time working up plans to combine our needs with his skill at meeting those needs within his field of expertise.

Because we had delegated many of our duties, the business continued to hum like a well-oiled machine, and we were able to keep our eye on things. During this period, we lost a few clinics to other dealers that were located closer to them geographically. We often wondered if there was a correlation in our being so preoccupied with the building and this unwelcome trend. Customer churn is inevitable in every business, however. We always hated to lose a customer. Even if the change was justifiable, it brought us a sense of loss. When a company grows to the size that ours had, losing a customer once in a while is expected. Still, it was hard for us to let go of them just as it was hard for us to let go of former employees. We had to remind ourselves constantly that this was a normal process, but we always used the experiences to add to our wisdom and continue to seek to serve our customers better. We started doing more and more PR calls to our customers, and they seemed to really appreciate this. Occasionally, we would make regular calls along with our employees. It never ceased to amaze and embarrass us that they made a big deal of our presence. That shows how important business relationships are in continuing customer relations. The two go naturally hand in hand.

In May, two weddings took place in the midst of all of the business happenings. After being widowed for sixteen years, Susan married Chuck Hiller, a wonderful man who is a pulmonary/critical care physician. Suddenly her family exploded—from one daughter to a total of two daughters, three sons, two daughters-in-law and 1.5 grandchildren!

My daughter married the talented programmer that came to work for us through our first acquisition. Not only had we gained an employee, but I had gained a son-in-law! Their wedding was held under a wedding tent in my backyard and the groom's father, an ordained minister, performed the ceremony. I inherited three more grandchildren in the process, and all family members were present for this wonderful celebration of life and love. Wow, what a year this had already been and how many emotions we had all experienced! Life was good and continued to be an exciting adventure for all of us.

Finally, the big day arrived for our groundbreaking ceremony— June 23, 1997. Once again, the Chamber of Commerce was there and many of our employees braved the hundred-plus temperatures of the day to attend. A representative from PCN was also present. It was indeed a magnificent day for all parties. I must admit that when I saw the temporary sign posted to the property identifying the owners, I felt my heart suddenly race at the possibility of a dream becoming a reality. So often in human experience, things don't seem real at the time, and it is only later that the experience tends to settle in and become fact, not fiction.

During that period, we seemed to grow even closer to our employees and appreciate them more. After all, they were going with us to the new building, and we had become very dependent on their particular skills and expertise. There were a few employees during that time who seemed to be especially endearing to us. For those, we are especially grateful. They know who they are. I will always be grateful for the long-term relationships and for the opportunity to mentor along the way.

One employee was a technical installer whom I had known for many years. He and my daughter had attended school together. I observed through his work that he was never going to become an outstanding technical employee. All our technical personnel not only had to be able to complete installations, but to diagnose and troubleshoot any problems between the hardware and the software. This man, however, loved to do landscaping and would head out the door hurriedly every day, especially in the summertime, to perform his "real love" of cutting lawns and improving the overall appearance of the outside surroundings. At some point, I became aware of his shortcomings in the installation process and knew a decision had to be made about his continued employment. I decided to talk with him and see what could be done. I needed to point out my feelings that he would be better served in pursuing his landscaping career instead of his technical one. I told him I felt he was never going to be outstanding in computers and that he should follow his heart and pursue his real love. Fortunately, he admitted that he wanted to go into landscaping full time. I advised him that he should do this and that I would be his first customer. It was the most unusual termination I ever conducted. Today, he is extremely successful and, yes, he still does my lawn.

In the early fall of 1997, we made a second acquisition, this one in Shreveport, Louisiana. Along with it came twenty-five more clients and a couple more employees. We decided to keep the office there open to foster continued local service and to support the customers. By purchasing two dealerships, we began to experience the growth spurts that only come through acquisitions. We increased our geographical status to three additional states with this latest purchase.

Electronic processing of claims continued to increase every time we added another state. Additionally, carriers seem to make it a practice to change their specifications on a frequent basis. Sometimes we felt they did this just to make our lives difficult, but of course we knew the changes were driven by government and state regulations. We now had installations in fourteen states and were required to keep up with each individual state's requirements. After much discussion, we decided to establish our own electronic clearinghouse in an effort to standardize as much as possible. The talents of a particular programmer and an especially capable electronic forms expert in our company made this possible. That gave us some time to change our standards within the company while not disrupting the cash flow of our doctors. Physicians were not at all understanding when glitches caused cash flow interruptions, and we were the first to hear about it. Of all the support problems and headaches associated with our business, this was by far the most difficult and time-consuming one. When our people got frustrated dealing with angry clients, I reminded them that it would be the same way if we held up their paychecks. After thinking about this statement, they always put their emotions and fatigue aside and dealt with fixing the problem at hand. Thank

God for capable people. I have no technical expertise, and working in this department would have stretched my patience level far beyond its capability.

Finally, the day arrived for us to move into our new home, our new building. It was November, 1997, and we were going to meet our deadline before the end of the year. Anyone who has ever built a house or participated in the building of a business structure can testify to how many frustrating hours are associated with the project. Builder's estimates are never on time, and why is it that the weather never cooperates when it is your project that is being held up? After months of meetings, dealing with stretched budgets, and the normal problems that always emerge, we were finally ready to make the new building our home. We felt very humbled, thankful, overwhelmed, and yes, a bit teary when thinking about the steps that had brought us to this place and point in time. Once again, God had allowed us to experience the fruits of our labor and our deepest desires in allowing all of this to happen.

We were all so excited the day of our move. Employee morale had never been higher. We actually had our own bathrooms, and yes, we could even cook in our own fully equipped kitchen. The building had 7,932 square feet of usable space. A favorite area was the huge seminar room which could be divided into two smaller rooms by utilizing the accordian wall. We had tried to consider all of our space requirements very carefully. Since we were planning to offer evening classes, we had carefully planned the entrance to be utilized without disrupting the administrative offices located on one side of the building or the support area located on the other.

Moving day went more smoothly than I had expected. Because of some proactive steps we had taken, our telephone system and cabling lines for our computers were already installed. The computers were housed in a special room, and over 150 cable lines were installed to meet existing and future needs of the company. I must say it was pretty impressive. Everyone was excited to occupy our new home. Teamwork and cooperation were at an all-time high the day we moved. No one even complained about having to load or unbox items to put into their individual workspaces. The tone was one of enthusiasm and expectancy as all went to their workspaces. We had tried to involve the employees in the process so that they had some say-so in determining how their work area was to be designed.

The month of December was utilized to the maximum with a grand opening ceremony which was attended by a huge crowd, including some PCN representatives who had traveled from New Jersey to help dedicate the building. Susan and I felt we were on top of the world! We had made it! We ran an article in our December newsletter which described this experience with "Don't just dream about it; do it!" There were more dreams, more plans, and more projects for the future. We felt that God wanted us to continue our journey through our business a while longer. We even had our Christmas party at our new building that year, and several creative employees did some amazing decorative touches which added to the festivities. It was a wonderful way to end the year.

Since the local newspaper had been unable to attend our grand opening in December, they offered to do an in-depth interview on our business. That was fine with us—the interview would provide much better public relations than we could ever have gotten on our own. The article came out in January, 1988, and the headline was, "Computer pioneers' business continues to evolve." There was also a very large color photo of Susan and me. The article briefly told our history and recounted some of the many experiences of our business. It also told of our move to our new headquarters. After that article, another one ran in a business-specific magazine. We were very grateful for the publicity, which really had a positive affect on our employees as well as our customers. Success has a way of breeding success, and people want to be a part of it. We all enjoyed ourselves during that period, and the publicity and praise added to everyone's individual self-confidence.

The year was filled with a flurry of business activity and new opportunities. As the business increased in size, keeping it on track became a constant challenge. Employee relations was a challenging part of this process. I have always said that managing people can sometimes be the most difficult part of the business, and yet, it is also the most important part. When you depend on people to help your business run efficiently, you must maintain cohesion and a good working environment. The more people, the more challenges. We now had thirty-three people working for us, and managing them properly had become a full-time job.

In February, we were notified by the magazine *Arkansas Business* that we were once again one of the finalists for Business of the Year, although in a different category than in 1992 since we had so many more employees. Even though we didn't win the competition, we were very honored to receive the nomination. It certainly helped our credibility, and we were featured in another article in the magazine. Once again, we received publicity and all benefited.

In the fall of that year, we had an opportunity to acquire another reseller. The company had been formed several months earlier from four separate ones that had merged. Many of their sites were located in some of the states in which we had installations and would provide penetration in added states. The company was experiencing financial difficulty and was laying off employees to cut costs. We struggled with this decision because it was by far the largest acquisition we would have done. The number of installations adopted would be more than 250. This would increase our total number to well over 550 total installations. It was a bold and gutsy move and would change the face of our company from a small to a mid-size business. We had already become one of the top dealers in the country, and this would make us an even larger entity. After several trips to the home office, we decided to proceed with the acquisition in November, 1998.

The added business not only brought us increased responsibilities, but it also placed a strain on our personnel. Adding a new business to an existing company is like merging two families together; there are a lot of personalities involved, and the rules and culture of each family are different. Our company had always tried to standardize all installations to make support from long distances easier through the use of the modem. Their company had many different types of hardware and software in their installations. Support of this kind was more difficult to maintain. Regardless of the circumstances, the combined entities became one big company. We had to make sure that all installations ran smoothly and that each individual clinic was able to maintain its regular office procedures.

Our existing employees were very nervous about taking on all of these installations. They weren't by themselves; Susan and I were aware that growth pains, if not managed carefully, can so disrupt a company that it cannot survive. Susan and I honestly felt that the acquisition was in the best interest of our company. We had thought long and hard about the opportunity and weighed many times the outcome of not taking it. We knew that we simply must continue to expand the company for the long-term security of our employees and for us, as well. Demands of employees for added perks and benefits were helping to drive this decision. If we were unable to meet these needs, we would be unable to retain our brightest and best employees.

There was also the challenge of dealing with a whole new set of personnel. They were located in several states, and the biggest task that lay ahead of us was trying to determine how to eliminate duplicate operations and cut overhead expenses. Because we were able to provide support from any location, we began to close offices that we felt were not being utilized and were not adding revenue to the bottom line of the operation. Next, there was the challenge of making sure that all customers were contacted and made to feel that we were going to improve the level of support they had been given, not lessen it. We had many years of experience by then, but it is always important to meet with customers on a face-to-face basis to introduce changes in management. We held free training seminars in larger locations and were able to meet the majority of the employees in a classroom setting. Additionally, we traveled to meet as many clinics that were unable to attend the seminars as we could. We wanted to make sure that the revenue stream we were receiving for support services was justified in the minds of our customers.

With this acquisition, we now had forty-five employees!

Our technical personnel visited as many sites as possible to ensure proper configurations of the systems we were supporting. This would also help to establish long-term relationships between our customers and our support personnel. Since we were approaching new industry standards for the year 2000, this made visits even more necessary. We had to be sure we were organized in our approach for the new year ahead. Many new industry standards were required for everyone to be Y2K ready, and we had to make sure we were on top of all of these requirements and that all of our customers were, also. Nothing prepared us for the New Year, however, with its added clinics and new requirements and the time it would take to get everything completed.

When January of 1999 rolled around, we found ourselves busier than ever. The word "crazy" could appropriately be used to describe the general mood. We were torn between loyalty to our old customers and our recently acquired ones. Each of our clinics had needs, and the support lines were busier than ever. Fortunately, we had purchased a new telephone system when we moved into our building, but we had to add additional upgrade modules to handle the increased load. Another T-1 line had to be added. We had one dispatcher who logged calls onto our electronic support help desk. With the increased level of calls, it was necessary to add another full-time dispatcher. The number of calls was increasing to more than one hundred per day. With clients from Colorado and Arizona to East Tennessee, the different time zones added more challenges. We started staggering the hours that our personnel worked to stretch out the hours we were available to help our customers. Needless to say, things were popping and, occasionally, tempers would flare. We spent most of our time making sure personnel were level. It was beginning to get frantic, and we hadn't even reached our busiest time of the year.

The year 1999 proved to be the most difficult year in our careers. Everyone in the computer industry as a whole was experiencing the same pressures. Almost every customer needed a minimum of software upgrades to make sure that the computers would recognize the new date of 2000. Years before, programmers had written programs that would not accommodate dates after December 31, 1999. Virtually any program that required mathematic calculations needed a computer chip that would recognize this new date. If electronic insurance claims were not filed within the required time period, little or no reimbursement could be received. One can see how important it was for the date to register properly.

We took inventory of our customers and divided them into different categories to determine the types of upgrades they would need. Some would only need minor upgrades, and some would need upgrades to operating systems. The older clients who did not have hardware that could handle the added software requirements would need to purchase new servers. Since many of our customers felt they were being unduly pressured, we spent a lot of time trying to educate them on technological facts that supported these requirements. Fortunately, the media helped support these claims because the term "Y2K" was on the minds of everyone. It was not a plan that we had devised to get more business; it was real. It did, however, provide for us the largest fiscal year in the history of our company.

The Y2K hype offered many challenges not only to our business but also to people in general. There were "doomsday" individuals who put fear in the hearts of others and tried to spread doubt that virtually anything electronic in businesses or in households would ever work properly at the beginning of the new year. Many of you remember how people bought extra supplies of water to alleviate possible shortages and the lack of electric power suggested by the press coverage. We even seriously considered buying a generator for fear that our own computer system would be unable to handle some of the unexpected things that might occur. We added to the frustration of our employees when we announced that we would have to delay vacation time during the month of December. By the end of the year, our personnel were getting tired, our customers had very little patience, and we were finding it hard to project a positive outward appearance to everyone. I remember going home exhausted, and on several occasions I went to bed too tired even to eat. I didn't want to talk to anyone, and when telephone solicitors called, I was even tempted to discontinue my phone service permanently.

Finally it was December 31, 1999, and—ready or not—it was going to happen. Because of a superb staff, we were as ready as we could be and had communicated the options to all of our customers. Almost everyone had purchased an upgrade of one type or another to meet the demands of the year 2000. A few were going to wait until the first quarter after the realization of how the date would affect their business. They had been too busy to have any downtime in their clinics and were willing to risk waiting another month or two. That was fine with us, for we were all very tired. Most people decided to spend a quiet evening ushering in the New Year, and we were all crossing our fingers in the hope that everything worked. The much-touted Y2K was approaching.

"A TIME TO..."

Susan and Ann speak:

Months before the appearance of the year 2000, a banner was placed in front of the Old Royal Observatory in Greenwich, England, exactly above the Prime Meridian that stated, "The Millennium Starts Here." In those same months, Y2K had become a familiar topic of conversation the world over. As mentioned in the previous chapter, in the early days of computers, storage space was at a premium. Programmers did all they could to conserve as much space as possible. It was important for them to use as few bits and bytes as feasible for the tasks to be performed. Someone had a brilliant space-saving idea: abbreviate all dates as six-numbers, two each for the day, month, and year. For the most part, this idea worked well.

In the intervening years, computer memory and storage became plentiful and economical. No longer was it necessary to write programs with such efficiency. This was good news; however, many, many pieces of software had already been written with six-digit dates. Suddenly someone realized, "Before long the year 2000 will be here. To enter the *current* date, not just one in the past, we will need an *eight*-digit date field." (It gets even more technical than that, but this is enough for this discussion.) The real issue was the element of the unknown: of the untold numbers of computers, which run everything from microwaves to airliners, which ones would and which ones would not be able to continue to function once the New Year arrived?

The world held its breath, and we in Little Rock were no

exception. We two knew well our profound dependence on computers. Not only did we use them to run our own business, they *were*
our business. Thinking back on the number of calls we received after each bad thunderstorm, we knew how much our clients relied
on them for their businesses.

One minute after 23:59 (GMT) it happened; 2000-01-01 arrived.
At 00:01 and then at 00:02, everything seemed to be intact and functioning, at least in England. What would happen in the rest of the
world? Three hours later Y2K arrived in Greenland and parts of South
America. In another hour, in eastern Canada. No panic or major problems yet, but it still hadn't gotten to Arkansas. At least within the next
hour, we could *see* what was happening. The huge crystal ball high
above Times Square was poised for its timely descent. All networks
carried the event and showed hordes crammed together for this ad-
vent celebration.

"Ten—nine—eight"...the ball crept downward..."three—two—
one—Happy New Year!" The television broadcast was still functioning; the famed lights of the Square were still shining; everything
seemed to be fine. We started to breathe a little more easily. Surely if
New York turned out OK, we would, too.

It was almost anticlimatic when midnight arrived in Arkansas,
but we were relieved. Many people have said that the Y2K panic and
hype turned out to be merely that, with no grounds for worry. Speaking specifically from our vantage point, we can say unequivocally that
the MOMS clients had a bare minimum of problems and disruptions
from the Y2K situation because of the Herculean efforts put forth
by our staff. As indicated before, they tested, retested, made modifications, and tested again. The clients who followed our advice were
the ones who were problem-free.

The Y2K was a non-event because, and only because, of the pre-
ventive preparations. Just as the date problem itself was a black eye
to the computer industry, the global cooperative efforts made to cor-
rect it were stars in its crown. There we were—2000 had arrived.

Once again, change was in the air. We knew it; we felt it and experienced a cold shudder. The probability of the acquisition of PCN
by a larger company was no secret. In order to obtain firsthand

knowledge of what was happening, what would be happening, and how we would fit into the picture, we decided to go to the PCN headquarters in New Jersey in mid-January and talk directly with those in charge. How many times we had been there before, as the offices fairly bustled with activity and excitement.

Pulling into the familiar parking lot, we giggled at the memory of the time when we each changed from professional to comfy travel clothes—in the car, right in that very spot. Then, we went around the building and up the stairs to the receptionist's desk. *Bam*, it hit us—where were all the people? Evidently, even more changes had been taking place than we knew. There were a few still there, but what a contrast to the numbers from the past. Somehow we did feel better when we saw our dear friend from Wallaby days and chatted with her. At least she was there.

During the course of the day, meetings with a number of the people who were still in charge of various parts of the company provided a little more information regarding future directions, or at least their "best guesses." Once acquisition took place it would be out of their hands.

At least we knew more when we left than when we arrived. However, one thing became evident to us both: this trip was being made for us to retrace our steps of so many years before. Sure, in the years in between we had both returned to New York several times, sometimes together. Again, this cold sense of change penetrated our beings, even more than the frigid January winds penetrated our bodies. Thus, we were determined—to make this a wonderful trip, to have some new experiences, and to revisit some favorite spots. We began by staying at our favorite hotel in a room overlooking Central Park, and proceeded with a morning stroll along Fifth Avenue, beside, then through, a bit of the Park. The Metropolitan Museum of Art was open by the time we arrived. We never miss it, nor the big salty pretzel with mustard bought from a vendor at the bottom of the Museum steps after we have torn ourselves from the exhibits. Times Square— a Broadway play—the little theater gift shop—Sardi's for a sip after the play.

"Do you remember the time we saw 'Victor-Victoria' and waited

in the cold right here at the stage door for Julie Andrews to appear?
We were inches from her!"

A wonderful trip it was, but what would the next months bring?

After returning from New York, we knew some decisions had
to be made. With the acquisition of PCN approaching, we began to
ask ourselves whether we needed to seek another product and work
once again toward "re-engineering" our business. A former employee
in another state had left MOMS and gone to work for a company
nearer his home. That company had written a comprehensive billing
package that integrated with a medical records product. It also had
the capability of running in a true Windows environment, and they
were working on a port to allow it to function over the Internet. The
company had called us at the request of the former employee and
asked whether we would be interested in seeing their product. Since
the company we currently represented was being purchased, we decided to see the product at their corporate headquarters. After all,
what could it hurt to look at something else?

We visited the software company, met with the principals, and
were totally impressed with their product. We felt their enthusiasm,
and it reminded us of the way we had felt in the early years of our
careers. When there is a spirit of passion in a company, it is quickly
spotted. They believed in their product, and all of their employees
expressed equal pride in it. They also seemed to possess the financial security that was necessary for us to consider them further. We
decided to obtain a demo of their software and take it back to show
to our employees.

Upon returning to MOMS, we gathered our managers together
for a brainstorming session and communicated the information from
our trip. Since the Y2K crisis was just barely over, we wondered what
their responses would be. Much to our surprise, they were exceed-
ingly enthusiastic. We had learned early in our business careers that
the most effective way to get others' interest is to allow them to be
part of the process. When employees are allowed to have input, they
will give their commitment to a project. Our business required the
skills and expertise of many people not only to make a product work,
but also to ensure that it flowed smoothly once it was installed. Team

cooperation was the only way to succeed.

After reviewing the product and asking many questions, it was obvious that our team leaders gave their thumbs up on marketing the new product. Our R & D department would begin to customize programs to meet Arkansas electronic claims requirements. Our plan was to begin marketing the product in our own state and then slowly expand to others. An electronic conversion would be required for each and every clinic that wanted to purchase it. This would require a great deal of time and effort. It was going to be much easier to sell the product than to do the technical modifications required to use it. Our company had always been able to "sell it" quicker than they could "build it."

Suddenly, the enormity of this task began to sink in. We had 550 customers. How long would it take to convert all of them, and would everyone want to buy the new product? Many of them had just spent a lot of money on Y2K upgrades; would they be willing to go to a different system so soon? How could we be sure that even if we made the decision to change software companies we would have an adequate market for it? These were the questions we were beginning to ask ourselves.

During the time we were going through this thought process, the corporation that was buying PCN contacted us. We knew what this meant: they were interested in acquiring us. After all, we were located in a key part of the country, one in which they had few installations and where we had become one of the largest dealers for our product. It seemed to be a natural supposition that they would try to purchase us. After much thought, we decided to talk with the representative. Our natural curiosity made us want to see what they had to say.

When the representative flew to Little Rock, we decided it would be wise to meet at a neutral location, our accountant's office. In this setting, if the value of our business came up in a discussion, we would be well prepared to provide more information. None of us was willing to proceed until both sides had signed Confidentiality Agreements. With this completed, the representative made his best sales pitch and talked to us about the overall picture of the computer healthcare industry. As we had felt earlier, he believed that physicians were going to be less likely to spend money on new systems and would be content to keep their current ones. They would be more likely to spend money on upgrades and other products to enhance and protect their existing investments. The overall strategy of this other company was going to be to keep the current customers happy and build toward an effective way to help reduce the paperwork nightmare that currently existed with insurance companies. They had an Internet port, which they envisioned assisting in this paperwork reduction task and helping to improve the overall efficiency of the physicians. Although the representative never exerted any heavy sales pressure on us, he very subtly gave us a ballpark amount of what they would be willing to pay to purchase us.

When the meeting was over, we asked our accountant to take the representative to the airport. We knew exactly what the discussion would be, and that they would be free to talk more openly out of our presence. Since our accountant also has an entrepreneurial personality and had worked with us for many years, we felt comfortable having him glean as much information as possible on our behalf.

True to form, our accountant contacted us and relayed their conversation. An offer was put on the table, and we needed to consider seriously whether or not we wanted to proceed. If we did, further discussions would be scheduled; but before that, we had our assignment. We needed to dedicate much time and prayer to considering this decision. It was by far the greatest of our professional careers and would have the most far-reaching effects of anything we had ever done. In the meantime, we had agreed to attend a conference in Florida the next week. This would give us some time to think about everything. A change of scene was exactly what we needed to help us evaluate all that had happened.

How appropriate for us to be going to Disney's Magic Kingdom! With all that was going on, we most definitely wanted and needed to escape. What better place than the land of make-believe?

Despite fantasy-world surroundings, we were in Orlando for a significant event. Several years before, we had both joined the

National Association of Women Business Owners (NAWBO) and had become very active on both the local and national levels. We realized that for twenty-five years this organization has remained true to its mission of strengthening its members, promoting economic development, creating effective changes within the business culture, building strategic alliances, and transforming public policy. A tall order, but an important one since there are more than eight million women-owned businesses in the United States, one-third of all U.S. businesses.

Both of us serve on the Board of the Central Arkansas Chapter and as representatives to the national Public Policy and Corporate and Economic Development councils. These positions required our attendance at the National NAWBO Convention, winter 2000, in Orlando. We were ready to go, but didn't realize how important those several days would be to us.

We used this time away from home to contemplate the decision before us. Since our company had been such a significant part of our lives for so many years, our first reactions bordered on mild, non-clinical depression. Perhaps "deflation" is a more accurate description. "If MOMS is sold, will this be our last NAWBO convention? What will we be? Who will we be?" On morning and afternoon walks around the nearby lake we were able to talk, to only each other, attempting to dissect the situation from all sides and all angles and to see what made sense and what did not. We walked and talked and walked and talked.

The first bright spot came when someone told us we had been NAWBO members long enough to qualify for continued membership whether or not the business was still ours. At least it would not be necessary to resign. Upon hearing this, we started gaining strength and perspective. There we were, surrounded by hundreds of capable, bright women. Each had accomplished something in the field of business, and so had we!

Another positive influence came when another WBO (woman business owner) related the fact that she had sold her business and had started another. Departure from the first did not signify the end of her productive life. In fact, she was having a lot more fun with the second than she did in the latter years of the first.

As always, there were many excellent seminars and workshops at the NAWBO convention. Attending a number of them inflated our enthusiasm even more. We still did not know where our next step would lead, but we did return from Orlando with our heads on much straighter than when we left.

After our return from the NAWBO conference, the feeling we had felt in Orlando remained. The change of scene had been great, and we began to realize that something was missing. Maybe we were just tired from the frenzied pace of the earlier months, but the feeling lingered for several days. Perhaps we both longed to pursue new horizons and weren't ready to admit it, even to ourselves. We both knew how much we enjoyed using our skills and experience to mentor and influence others. The idea of re-engineering our business and perhaps making it an even larger company did not have the appeal it once had, however. We had made our mark; what purpose would it serve to continue on this path?

As emphasized throughout this writing, we have both known for many years the true Source of our strength and direction. At this point, though, we alternately agonized, prayed, talked, and, yes, cried. Since the answers still did not seem clear, we wrestled with the various possibilities and the probable results of each. We prayed more, talked more, and, yes, cried more.

True to His faithfulness, God provided a breakthrough with a powerful sermon. After reading from the third chapter of Ecclesiastes, the minister spoke of there being a time and a season for all things. He stated that change was a constant in our lives but that God always helps us through those changes if we ask for His help and guidance. Once again we knew from experience that this was true. We truly needed His help and guidance.

Although the author of Ecclesiastes is not mentioned by name, evidence points to Solomon, purportedly a very wise man. The book explores the futility of man's dependence on wealth, pleasure, or even human wisdom. It indicates that a truly wise man lives his life in obedience to God. Even though we do learn from our own personal experiences, our wisdom increases as we look to God and attempt to obey His will in the events and decisions that make up these experiences of our lives.

"God, what *are* you trying to tell us?"

Ann speaks:

Several years before Bill's death, I was involved in the interdenominational Bible Study Fellowship, founded in the 1940s by an English lady, A. Wetherell Johnson. Born into a wealthy family, she was educated in Europe during the 1920s and exposed to agnosticism, which she subsequently adopted as part of her beliefs. Through an unexpected turn of fate, she was held in a Japanese internment camp near Shanghai during World War II. During this stay, she became a Christian and later established the BSF, which became the largest Bible study organization in the world.

I was so profoundly influenced by the life of this lady and the program she had designed that I studied it diligently every week for more than five years. One lesson was especially meaningful to me. It provided a very practical method for making decisions:

- Pray for direction in the decision-making process.
- Look for the indicators or signs that seem to indicate what you need to do.
- Wait for the peace for having made the decision.

I have since added a fourth element: "sleep on a decision" before following through with it. Somehow the dawn of a new day can add a perspective that the day before did not reveal. Soon after forming our business, I shared these steps with Susan and later with many of our employees. Decisions? Four steps to resolution.

Susan speaks:

Rarely do I drive a car without having the radio tuned to an NPR station. In my many miles of travel and being in so many different cities, it is a comfort to discover the familiarity of this network of stations, all in the same part of the dial. One particular morning, unable to locate the Houston NPR, I turned to the local Christian station.

The hotel where I was staying was not far from the office building where I would be meeting that day. This was to be a very important session, the results of which could heavily influence whether we did or did not land a multi-site contract. Being the only MOMS person there, I knew well the responsibility on my shoulders. Usually calm, I admittedly was allowing a little trepidation to creep into my emotions. With thoughts aimed toward the upcoming meeting, I was paying little attention to the radio—until I realized which selection had just begun. "Great is Thy faithfulness...all that I needed Thy hand has provided...Great is Thy faithfulness, Lord unto me."

My spirit was calmed because I was reminded that He would be beside me during that presentation. He was, but since that time I have realized over and over again how God uses that song and Lamentations 3:23, the verse of Scripture on which it is based, to speak to me in times of fear or uncertainty. He doesn't just bring it to my mind but allows me to be someplace where it is being sung or read.

During the time when Ann and I were trying to make this huge decision, Chuck and I were in a church service. My tears began streaming as voices chimed, "Great is Thy faithfulness...Lord unto me." I knew that He would be faithful if we, indeed, looked to Him for guidance in this decision.

Ann and Susan speak:

Ecclesiastes 3:1—"To every thing there is a season, and a time for every purpose under the heaven."

Lamentations 3:23b—"Great is Thy faithfulness."

The four steps to making decisions according to God's will.

We had the tools and the direction. The passage from Ecclesiastes seemed to be telling us that perhaps our "season of business" needed to end, and a new season needed to emerge. Maybe God truly did have new horizons He wanted us to discover. We had often told others that our greatest hope was that once we were no longer affiliated with our business, we wanted nothing more than for it to continue. This would provide even further proof that this, which we had created, was bigger than ourselves. It would be considered ultimate success if, when we were no longer required to be associated with it, it could stand alone.

Suddenly, we had our answer. We needed to "let go of the lesser to obtain the greater." There were new fields to conquer and new opportunities to explore. This experience was a building block for future endeavors. God had allowed us to journey along this path through our pain and create something wonderful as a result. By "letting go and letting God," we would be able to discover His new paths for our lives. We were sure that we would be given the answers if we asked the questions and waited for the ultimate wisdom that He would give us.

"We sell."

We prayed; we looked for the indications or signs that our decision was right; we felt a peace; and we waited another day to be sure.

"Yes, we sell."

"Dear God, great *is* Your faithfulness!"

"It is now time to..."

MOMS Valley Press
www.MOMSvalley.com
P. O. Box 241057
Little Rock, AR 72223-0001